U2

U2

Jackie Shirley

LONGMEADOW
P R E S S

This 1993 edition published by
Longmeadow Press
201 High Ridge Road
201 High Ridge Road
Stamford CT 06904

Produced by
Brompton Books Corporation
15 Sherwood Place
Greenwich, CT 06830

ISBN 0-681-41875-3

Printed in Hong Kong

0 9 8 7 6 5 4 3 2 1

PAGE 1: Guitarist Dave 'The
Edge' Evans, bass-player
Adam Clayton, drummer Larry
Mullen, and vocalist Paul
'Bono' Hewson in Paris during
the $35-million grossing 1987
world tour following the
release of their breakthrough
album, *The Joshua Tree*.

PAGES 2-3: In the early days in
Dublin the band and manager
Paul McGuinness would spend
hours discussing how they
would take over the world.
That was exactly what they
seemed to have done in the
summer and fall of 1987.

PAGES 4-5: Bono in
performance; he has described
himself as the 'heart of the
band, The Edge is the head,
and Larry and Adam are the
legs.' Bono's high profile was
to attract criticism in the wake
of *The Joshua Tree*.

What makes a rock band legendary, rather than merely memorable? What distinguishes those whose star will continue to ascend from those who will shine brightly but briefly, or those who will simply fade slowly into oblivion? Is it timing, luck, genuine originality and creativity, a single-minded hunger to succeed, or mere media manipulation? Perhaps it is a combination of some or all of these things. Perhaps it simply eludes definition. Perhaps the closest we can come to understanding it is when we see it happening with our own eyes. Two billion people saw it happening with U2 at the Live Aid extravaganza to raise funds for the starving of Ethiopia on 13 July 1985.

The four Dubliners – singer Paul 'Bono' Hewson, guitarist Dave 'The Edge' Evans, bassist Adam Clayton, and drummer Larry Mullen – were a band for whom great things were predicted. After years of slumming it in the back of tour buses across Britain, Europe, and America, they were finally riding high on the crest of the big-league wave. Their last two albums had stormed into the British charts at #1 and they had climbed to the upper reaches of the singles charts with singles like *Pride (In the Name of Love)* and *The Unforgettable Fire*. America's *Rolling Stone* magazine had named them as the band most likely to dominate the Eighties.

But on that day in July they were just the latest sensation tucked away in a line-up that included some of the greatest stars that rock and pop had ever produced – Mick Jagger and David Bowie, Tina Turner, Elton John, Queen, Sting, Dire Straits. Bob Dylan would sing via a satellite link from Philadelphia, The Who and Led Zeppelin had both reformed especially for the show, and Paul McCartney would close it with *Let it Be*.

U2's slot was at 5pm. They had 20 minutes – maximum. Organizer and fellow Dubliner Bob Geldof was running a tight ship. Nobody could overrun and no fans would be allowed on stage. They started with *Sunday, Bloody Sunday,* went into *Bad* and planned to finish with their anthemic hit single, *Pride (In the Name of Love).*

Bad was an adaptable track, Bono would often improvise by sweeping into *Ruby Tuesday, Walk on the Wild Side*, and *Sympathy for the Devil.* But today there was something especially manic about the way he restlessly roamed the huge stage, like a caged lion. He ventured to the front of the stage and held out his microphone to the audience. The response was ecstatic. Now he was motioning to a girl a few rows back to come to him. The rest of the band hid their bewilderment – and frustration – as they carried on playing. The girl started pushing through to the stage but was held back by the security guards. Still Bono was gesturing. Still the band kept playing. Precious seconds were ticking by.

Backstage U2 manager Paul McGuinness was looking anxiously at his watch. Soon there wouldn't be time for a third song. What was Bono playing at? And at something this BIG!

But Bono was determined. He shouted at the security men to help her through, then leapt from the stage into the pit separating the crowd from the stars. McGuinness was apoplectic. Hardly any of the 72,000 people in Wembley Stadium could see what was going on, all they could hear was the repetitiveness of the band as they struggled to fill in until Bono brought the girl on stage to slow-dance. By the time he closed the song they had been playing *Bad* for 14 minutes. They waved goodbye and ran off stage. 'We really thought we had blown it,' admitted The Edge.

Bono, particularly, later confessed to being inconsolable

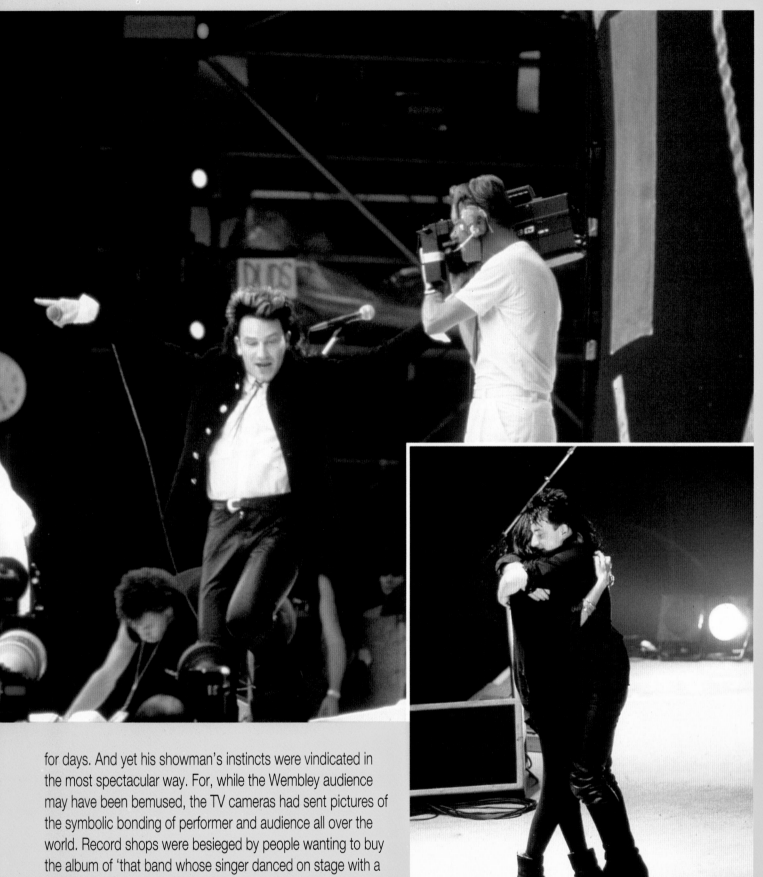

for days. And yet his showman's instincts were vindicated in the most spectacular way. For, while the Wembley audience may have been bemused, the TV cameras had sent pictures of the symbolic bonding of performer and audience all over the world. Record shops were besieged by people wanting to buy the album of 'that band whose singer danced on stage with a girl from the audience'. Bono's antics could have been seen as a gimmicky, self-seeking breach of the spirit of Live Aid. Instead U2 were hailed as heroes, a band who had gone for the emotional jugular and won. Bono's gesture was seen as second only to the brilliant showmanship of the late Freddie Mercury.

At 5pm on 13 July there were high hopes. By 5.20pm there was no doubt . . . U2 were the band of the Eighties.

INSET: **Bono embraces a girl from the audience; the ultimate 'contact' performer, at Live Aid he ignored Bob Geldof's 'no fans on stage' instructions to indulge in symbolic bonding.**

MAIN PICTURE: **A cameraman films Bono as he wins over the live audience for 'Live Aid.'**

Hailed as 'radical' and 'exciting' when it opened in the summer of 1972, Mount Temple was indeed a very different kind of Irish school. Conceived in an era of post-Sixties optimism, it was the first non-denominational, co-educational comprehensive school in Dublin. The emphasis was on individual growth and fulfillment, rather than collective academic excellence. Personal creativity was encouraged, not stifled, uniforms were out, girls mixed freely with boys, Catholics with Protestants.

It was in this heady, free-thinking, anything-is-possible atmosphere that the four very different young men who would eventually become U2 met toward the end of 1976.

The instigator was Larry Mullen. He was 15, blond, good looking in a Seventies' teen-idol kind of way, and had been playing the drums since the age of 9. He came from a close-knit, lower middle-class family who lived in the Dublin district of Artane. Larry's mother was a typist who loved to play the piano and young Larry had taken piano lessons too until he managed to persuade his parents that he would do chores around the house if they paid for him to have lessons with Ireland's best-known drummer, Joe Bonnie. He played in the St Patrick's Day parade in O'Connell Street with the Post Office Workers' Band.

But young Larry nurtured other dreams. Using a drum pad, he would mimic the bands on the BBC Television show *Top of the Pops*. When his mother finally bought him a drum kit for £17 ($35) he was in no doubt. He decided to pin a note on the Mount Temple noticeboard to see if anyone else shared his dream of *being* one of the bands on *Top of the Pops*. His note referred to 'money wasted on a drum kit' and asked 'are there others out there who, perhaps, have done the same on guitars?' The only interest came from a fellow pupil he vaguely knew called Dave Evans.

Dave was an unlikely prototype rock star – quiet, earnest, academically inclined. He had been born in Barking, East London but his Welsh Presbyterian parents had lived in the middle-class Dublin suburb of Malahide since he was a baby. Both parents played the piano, and his father was a founder member of the Dublin Welsh Male Voice Choir. As a teenager Dave had taken piano and Spanish guitar lessons. With his older brother, Dick, who had made his own electric guitar, he would knock out old Beatles songs. He was uncertain of his future but intrigued enough to contact Larry.

Larry, meanwhile, was keen to enlist another fellow pupil, Adam Clayton. Adam was a misfit, even in a school which prided itself on unconventionality. He had a public schoolboy English accent, and his parents, an ex-RAF pilot and an air hostess, were erroneously reputed to be filthy rich. They lived, like the Evanses, in Malahide. Destined for Eton or

NO FEEDBACK

Harrow then Oxbridge, Adam had proved an exasperating, quietly rebellious child and his parents had compromised by sending him to St Columba's College, about six miles from Dublin. Constantly in trouble for laziness and truancy, he eventually transferred to Mount Temple.

He dressed like a bohemian – caftans and shaggy coats, a kilt sometimes and dark glasses always. He never did any homework. He was a disaster, but impossible to dislike. He would confound even his teachers by explaining, in perfectly polite and impeccably enunciated tones: 'I know this is awkward, sir. I am very sorry about it but there is nothing I can do. I simply don't understand this stuff, sir.'

Privately he was more concerned about his failures. He had decided – with no particular justification – that he would become 'the greatest bass guitarist in the world.' He strummed along occasionally with a local band called the Max Quad Band and impressed his schoolfriends with talk of 'gigs' and 'frets' and 'feedback.' Besides, he owned an amplifier. He joined Larry, Dave, and Dave's brother Dick – soon to join another once-promising band, The Virgin Prunes.

All they were missing was a singer. Then Adam thought of Paul Hewson . . .

Paul was also something of an oddity at Mount Temple. His mother had died very suddenly after suffering a brain haemorrhage at her father's funeral. The tragedy had a profound effect on the troubled teenager. Almost overnight he changed his appearance – turning up with a spiky red haircut, tight purple jeans, pointed boots, a Sixties' jacket, a chain from nose to ear . . . and an attitude. He flourished at art, music, history, and English. He chased girls, got drunk, went 'mooning,' flirted with starting a drama troupe, and hung

LEFT: An early publicity photo from the days when U2 were drawing loyal crowds at home but had yet to break Britain.

9

ABOVE LEFT: Larry Mullen – it was he who started it all.

RIGHT: The Edge – guitar hero in the making.

ABOVE RIGHT: Adam who hustled for gigs in the early days.

FAR RIGHT: Ever the poser, Bono in the late seventies.

around with a group of arty bohemians who called themselves the Lypton Village and prided themselves on doing outrageous things – like wearing make-up in the street.

But he was full of contradictions, and seemed to be floundering without any real sense of direction. There was a serious side to him as well. He played chess in the All-Ireland Games, for example, and he had a deep need to explore his spiritual side. He was the child of a mixed marriage – his father Catholic, his mother a Protestant – and they lived comfortably in Dublin's Northside. Paul could not settle for either religion fully. He was fleetingly impressed by the Plymouth Brethren but, after his mother's death, his need for spiritual solace grew and he joined the school's Christian Union.

Bono agreed to meet with the others anyway for the 'audition' to be held in Larry's kitchen in Rosemount Avenue, Artane. The four were not, at first, natural bedfellows. They had oddly contrasting personalities and their musical tastes were very different, save for a common love of Bowie and The Stones. Larry liked David Essex and The Sweet, Paul was into Sixties' rock and roll and Elvis, while Dave liked Rory Gallagher, Taste, the Beatles and Yes. They ran through a couple of Stones' classics, *Brown Sugar* and *Satisfaction*.

One thing was clear – Larry and Dave could actually play their instruments. Dave secured the place of lead guitarist with a searing rendition of the Taste classic, *Blister on the Moon*. Adam, however, for all his talk and posing, was struggling. But he looked right, and was worldly and confident. And desperate . . . I'd failed at everything else so I just had to make a success of this,' he later admitted. And Paul? Well, he'd said he could play guitar when he obviously couldn't. He was loud and opinionated and couldn't sing much either, but he had conviction and that indefinable something, a kind of presence. They decided to give it a go. Their name, for the time being anyway, would be Feedback.

Encouraged by Temple's dedicated music teacher, Albert Bradshaw, Feedback agreed to practice three times a week. They were not writing their own material then and were barely able to get through the endless covers of The Stones, Bowie, The Moody Blues, and Elvis.

But they had little else to do. Even Paul, whose enthusiasm had wavered as he studied for his Leaving Certificates exam in order to secure a university place, was now fully committed. A bureaucratic error had seen him admitted to Dublin's University College only to be thrown out days later when it was discovered that he had not passed the compulsory entrance exam in Gaelic.

The band now had several new names. Paul had allegedly nicknamed Dave 'The Edge' because of his prominent chin. Paul himself was now known as Bono. Stories vary as to how this weird name came about. Some say it was taken, on a whim, from the name of a hearing-aid shop in O'Connell Street. Other rumors, which sound more likely, say it came from the Latin for good voice – 'Bono vox.' Soon they would drop Feedback in preference for The Hype. Their first gig was at a talent contest organized by Mount Temple. They sounded rough, but their energy was infectious. They performed Peter Frampton's *Show Me the Way*, a parody of the Bay City Rollers, and a Beach Boys' medley. They won. Adam, particularly, was ecstatic. He talked of 'getting a good manager,' making a demo tape,' 'going on the road' . . . Bono would later refer to this gig as 'the greatest one we ever did. We could only play three chords but we knew there was an excitement when we were playing. We built U2 round a spark, that's the only secret to U2.'

Their second gig was at St Fintan's School in the middle-class district of Sutton, playing support for a Dublin band long since forgotten. They added some Stones' and Boomtown Rats' numbers to their Mount Temple set. Word had it that Bono was a bit of a 'prat,' that he hurled himself into the audience, that he lacked the mean, moody, detached sexiness of big-time contemporary Irish rock stars like Geldof fronting the Rats and Phil Lynott of Thin Lizzy. But the sheer passion and sincerity of his performance was undeniable. Almost despite themselves, the Saturday disco crowd were won over by the gauche, manic lead singer of The Hype.

Perhaps fortuitously, Adam had been thrown out of Mount Temple. He had been caught streaking down a corridor. It was one rebellion too many. His parents worried about his future, he worried about The Hype. While the other band members studied, he became the unofficial manager – getting the No 42 bus into town each day to hustle for gigs. Every gig mattered but some mattered more than most. Dublin's burgeoning rock scene revolved around the square mile centered on Grafton Street.

Adam spent his days hanging around in gig-land, chatting up the people who mattered at the Baggot Inn, McGonagles, Moran's Hotel, the Project Arts Centre, and The Celebrity Club. He was quick to spot how important pirate DJ Dave Fanning and independent music paper *Hot Press* would become to U2 and he lobbied them heavily. Miraculously both

came to the fore just when the band needed them in those make-or-break months of 1978.

It was Adam who spotted the advert for the Harp and Guinness Talent Contest in Limerick, to be held on 18 March 1978. They had already played one gig the night they went on. Bono was hoarse and their set was nowhere near as polished as the other competitors. But still the magic was there. As Bono recalled: 'We were a shambles. But I knew we had something, I could feel the effect we had on the audience. The important thing was that we worked around that spark. We were stumbling in the dark, but with the spark and fanning it.' They won the first prize of £500 and the chance to audition for CBS Ireland.

Emboldened by this latest triumph Adam became even more daring in his lobbying. He would pose as a friend, or record company executive, or a concert promoter to elicit the home telephone numbers of rock stars from their unsuspecting families - anything to be able to speak directly to those whose advice and patronage could help. An early victim was Gerry Cott, lead guitarist with the Rats. When Thin Lizzy were playing in Dublin, Adam managed to break through the red tape to talk to Phil Lynott in his hotel bedroom at 6am. Lynott listened wearily but his advice was succinct: 'Get a manager, get a good demo, send it to everyone in London.'

Adam also began sounding people out about a new name for the band. Names with initials or numbers were in vogue – UB40, XTC. Someone suggested U2. U2 was the colloquial name given to American intelligence planes during the Cold War, made famous when the Soviets shot down American pilot Gary Powers and produced him as a spy in Moscow in 1960. 'It's perfect. You don't know what it means but it sticks with you,' said Adam.

Next, with Lynott's advice ringing in his ears, Adam contacted Bill Graham, a writer on *Hot Press* who had long championed the young band's cause. They desperately needed a good manager, was there anyone he could suggest? Graham thought for a moment. He knew this was potentially a crucial development for U2.

Eventually it hit him. 'Why don't you try getting Paul McGuinness . . .'

LEFT: The Edge was an unlikely prototype rockstar – quiet, earnest, and academically inclined. He had been born in East London, but had lived with his Welsh Presbyterian parents in a middle-class suburb of Dublin since he was a baby. He earned his place in the embryonic U2 with a searing rendition of the Taste classic 'Blister on the Moon.'

RIGHT: The 'baby band' in Dublin; in the Mount Temple days they called themselves Feedback and performed endless if unremarkable covers of the Stones, Bowie, The Moody Blues, and Elvis. They soon dropped that name in preference for The Hype and only became U2 (in keeping with the band names containing initials of numbers that were in vogue in the late seventies, like UB40 and XTC) when someone mentioned the coloquial name given to American spy planes during the cold war. 'It's perfect. You don't know what it means, but it sticks with you,' said Adam.

Just why Paul McGuinness's name sprang to Bill Graham's lips that day remains something of a mystery. A squadron leader's son, educated by Jesuits and then at Trinity College, Dublin, McGuinness had had a varied, and not always successful, career to date. He had dabbled in advertising, run a failed mobile disco, and enjoyed a brief moment of glory by persuading forgotten Sixties' singer Donovan to come out of retirement to perform in Ireland.

He had also driven a mini-cab, been a tour guide to Lourdes, and worked as a location manager on a movie starring Sean Connery. Apart from the Donovan coup his only experience of the rock business was a brief period as manager to an Irish folk band called Spud.

Adam, of course, knew nothing of this and set about netting the man he now believed held the key to international success for U2. He bombarded McGuinness with phone calls. McGuinness sounded skeptical. He arranged meetings. McGuinness always seemed to have a last-minute, 'cannot-be-avoided' alteration to his schedule. Adam lined up gigs. McGuinness didn't show. The band members were becoming increasingly desperate. Though their families tried to be supportive, ferrying them around to gigs, helping to finance the purchase of equipment and so on, they were, not unnaturally, worried that their sons should begin to think about what to do with their lives rather than invest all their hope in U2.

Larry, The Edge, Bono, and Adam – especially Adam – clung on. They had put their hearts and souls into U2, they were improving vastly as musicians, they were beginning to write their own material, they had rapturous receptions wherever they played, and they had Dave Fanning (the influential Dublin DJ) and *Hot Press* (the influential Dublin music paper) on their side. They couldn't give up now just when stardom was beckoning so tantalisingly. They didn't – and on 25 May 1978 Paul McGuinness finally came to see them as a support band at The Project.

McGuinness had the air of a man who was fulfilling just another obligation as he sat reading a newspaper during the set by the headliners, a band called Revolver. But he soon put it down when U2 came on stage. For a start, he noticed, they ran on stage. It was fast becoming the fashion, with punk and the New Wave, for bands to amble on and stage and affect a cool indifference to the audience. U2 were anything but cool. The drummer was solid, the guitarist, playing a heavy, angular Gibson, was undoubtedly gifted, the bass guitarist . . . well, he definitely looked the part and could keep up a fascinating rhythm. And the singer . . . ? He was utterly compelling. He couldn't sing but what energy, what courage. He had a showman's intuition, he worked the audience, he was unafraid of looking foolish, he would win the crowd over with his sheer

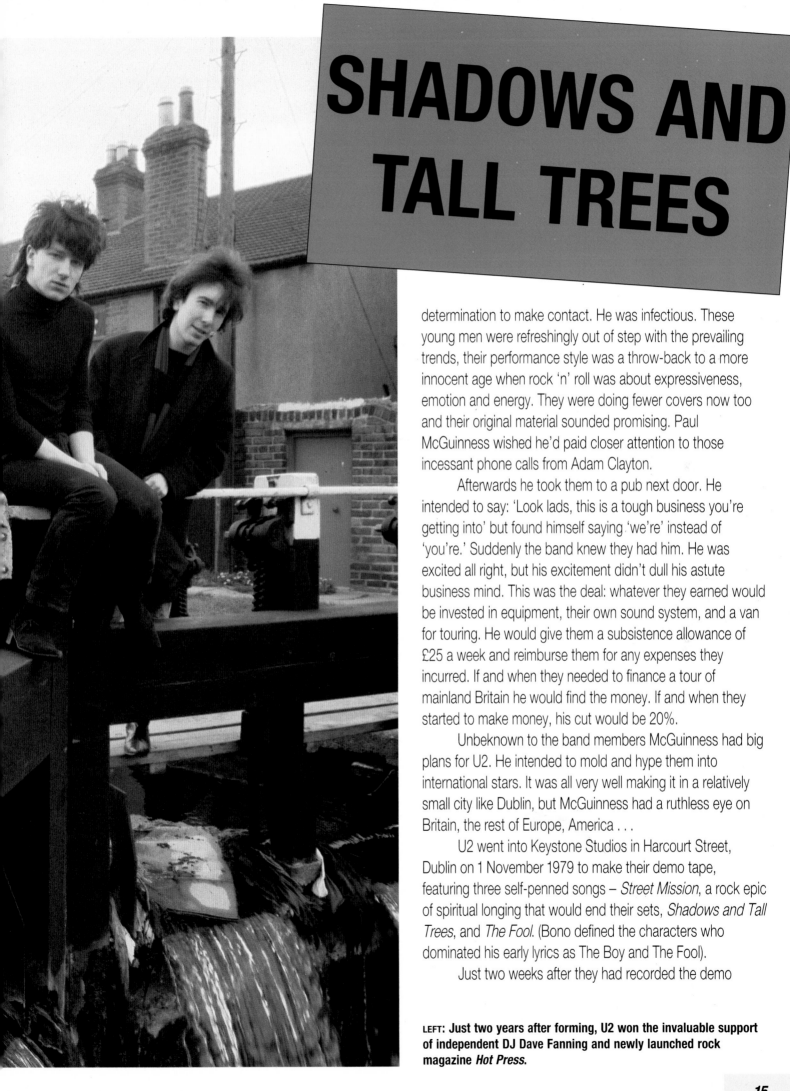

SHADOWS AND TALL TREES

determination to make contact. He was infectious. These young men were refreshingly out of step with the prevailing trends, their performance style was a throw-back to a more innocent age when rock 'n' roll was about expressiveness, emotion and energy. They were doing fewer covers now too and their original material sounded promising. Paul McGuinness wished he'd paid closer attention to those incessant phone calls from Adam Clayton.

Afterwards he took them to a pub next door. He intended to say: 'Look lads, this is a tough business you're getting into' but found himself saying 'we're' instead of 'you're.' Suddenly the band knew they had him. He was excited all right, but his excitement didn't dull his astute business mind. This was the deal: whatever they earned would be invested in equipment, their own sound system, and a van for touring. He would give them a subsistence allowance of £25 a week and reimburse them for any expenses they incurred. If and when they needed to finance a tour of mainland Britain he would find the money. If and when they started to make money, his cut would be 20%.

Unbeknown to the band members McGuinness had big plans for U2. He intended to mold and hype them into international stars. It was all very well making it in a relatively small city like Dublin, but McGuinness had a ruthless eye on Britain, the rest of Europe, America . . .

U2 went into Keystone Studios in Harcourt Street, Dublin on 1 November 1979 to make their demo tape, featuring three self-penned songs – *Street Mission*, a rock epic of spiritual longing that would end their sets, *Shadows and Tall Trees*, and *The Fool*. (Bono defined the characters who dominated his early lyrics as The Boy and The Fool).

Just two weeks after they had recorded the demo

LEFT: **Just two years after forming, U2 won the invaluable support of independent DJ Dave Fanning and newly launched rock magazine *Hot Press*.**

Larry's mother, Maureen Mullen, was killed in a road accident in Raheny. Larry was inconsolable, his mother had also been his staunchest supporter, his closest confidante. The tragedy brought him closer to Bono who had lost his own mother in similarly sudden circumstances. Not long after this three of the band members would enter into something that would promote controversy and conflict later on. Bono had kept up his friendships from the Lypton Village days. Many of his former inner circle had become interested in a charismatic Christian group called Shalom. They belonged to a generation increasingly disillusioned with the strictures of Catholicism. Dublin itself was a breeding ground for a proliferation of 'alternative' religious groups. It wouldn't be long before Bono would persuade The Edge and grief-stricken Larry to join Shalom.

Paul McGuinness took the demo tape to tout around London. Nobody was interested. This was an era dominated

RIGHT: **Feigning indifference for the cameras in the tried-and-tested rock tradition in Dublin.**

BELOW: **When Paul McGuinness first saw them live he had the air of a man fulfilling an obligation. At the end of the set he wished he had paid more attention to those incessant phone calls from Adam Clayton.**

by the noise of punk, the catchy irritation of novelty songs, the bland perfection of ballads, and the emergence – in Britain anyway – of the New Romantics, personified briefly by the tribal chants and exotic costumes of bands like Adam and the Ants. U2 and their blend of emotional lyrics and raw-energy guitars just didn't fit in. McGuinness was disappointed but not deterred. A different tactic was called for. Although the band members had turned down the original CBS deal after winning the Harp Talent Contest in Limerick, McGuinness now went back to the company's Irish supremo, Jackie Hayden.

He shrewdly negotiated a record deal that was for Ireland only and would allow the band to pursue other arrangements elsewhere. But there were tensions in the band. Bono, particularly, was frustrated by McGuinness. They were gigging like crazy, they were being spoken of in the Irish music Press as if they were the new saviors of Irish rock, and yet this whizzkid manager couldn't even line them up a better deal than one they had already turned down themselves in 1978.

Almost as if he couldn't accept the rejection Bono went off himself to hawk the demo round every rock critic in

London. When he returned, similarly chastened, he was perhaps in a better mood to appreciate what would be the first of many strokes of marketing genius from McGuinness.

Only 1000 numbered copies of the band's first single would be pressed – enough to get a #1 single in Ireland. Bono and The Edge would appear on Dave Fanning's new 'legit' radio show on RTE where, in a unique participation stunt, three different tracks would be played and listeners would be invited to choose the A-side. The three chosen songs were

ABOVE: From the start Bono had a showman's intuition and could win over a crowd with sheer determination and energy, thought McGuinness.

RIGHT: Adam Clayton – having failed everything else he had set his heart on being a rock star. But he would have difficulties later coping with the evangelical Christianity of Bono, The Edge, and Larry.

Stories for Boys, a live favorite, *Boy-Girl,* and *Out of Control.*

Out of Control won and the limited-edition single, *U2:3,* featuring all tracks, was produced by Chas de Whalley. The lyrics – 'I was feeling out of control, I had a crazy notion it was out of control' – were said to reflect Bono's continuing inner confusion over his mother's sudden death. He himself said it was about an adolescent realization that 'the two most important decisions in your life had nothing to do with you – being born and dying.' The song became a U2 favorite, opening and closing their shows, and it topped the Irish charts in September 1979.

The success of the single gave the band some comfort. But money was still a worry. Other bands were earning £600-£700 a week playing residences, headlining at McGonagles, the Baggot Inn, Moran's Hotel. U2 were lucky to make £300 in a fortnight. McGuinness, for reasons best known to himself, was keeping them on a tight leash. They didn't take residences, they only did 'special' events – gigs that were widely publicized and had the feel of exclusivity. It was all very well but they had to live . . . McGuinness would sit in his office reading the *Irish Times* while the band cadged their bus fares home from his small-change jar. In the watering holes of Grafton Street Dublin's rock cognoscenti were gossiping maliciously about the manipulative powers of the rich English bastard who managed U2.

Still bitter Bono took it upon himself to approach John Fisher. Fisher owned a badge stall in the Dandelion Market at the top of Grafton Street and had started to stage gigs in his large storage shed on Saturday and Sunday afternoons. Many of U2's most loyal fans were too young to attend pub gigs at the Baggot or McGonagles. Dandelion Market proved ideal for them and, though the band only ever played four or five gigs there the buzz was out and youngsters flocked to them from all over Dublin.

McGuinness, meanwhile, announced that U2 would shortly undertake a brief tour playing some of the most prestigious venues in London. He hinted, too, that an international recording contract was 'imminent,' at this, the end of a year in which U2 had seen unprecedented success, breaking through with their first single, appearing on radio and television, and winning the coveted spot on the cover of *Hot Press.*

The 'international recording contract' hint stemmed from his success in securing a promise from two senior London-based EMI executives to come to Dublin to hear U2. McGuinness was thrilled. This could be the big break they were waiting for. The two would see his band on their home ground, playing to an already converted crowd and riding high on the success of *Out of Control.*

FAR LEFT: **Larry's beloved mother, Maureen, was tragically killed in a road accident just two weeks after the band had recorded their first demo tape on 1st November 1979. Griefstricken he sought consolation in the Dublin charismatic Christian group Shalom.**

LEFT: **Bono, also a member of Shalom, could relate easily to Larry's suffering. His own mother had died from a brain haemorrhage while he was still at Mount Temple.**

ABOVE: **After scratching around for gigs, the band had their first taste of success after winning the Harp and Guinness talent contest in Limerick in March 1978. They won £500 and the chance to audition for CBS Ireland.**

The gig would be at the Baggot Inn. It had a low roof, only held about 200 people, and stank of booze, urine, and sweat. But it was intimate and atmospheric, an ideal backdrop for a making-contact-with-the-audience singer like Bono. Word of the London visitation had spread fast and the place was full long before the starting time of 8.30pm. The EMI men duly arrived and took their VIP seats. Backstage, McGuinness told the band to 'go for it.' They hit the stage running and blazed through a set that contained all their audience-grabbers, *Out of Control, Shadows and Tall Trees, Concentration Cramp, In Your Hand,* and *The Fool*.

The audience went wild. McGuinness was happy. His boys had lived up to and beyond his expectations. But then, with the set only halfway through, he noticed the EMI men get up to leave. Sorry, they whispered as they brushed past him, we've got to get back to the hotel to see The Specials on the *Old Grey Whistle Test* (a cult BBC rock show).

The band carried on oblivious. When, during the encores, Bono noticed the record executives had disappeared he assumed they were backstage making a deal with McGuinness. When they were told the truth they were close to despair. McGuinness was too, but he had to keep them buoyed up. The London tour, he said, could be the break they needed. Gigs had been lined up at some of the capital's hottest venues. There was even the possibility of playing support to Talking Heads.

U2 left for their first trip to London in December 1979. On the eve of departure a publishing deal McGuinness had lined up to finance the cost of the band and their three-man crew had suddenly collapsed. The trip was saved at the last minute with loans from the boy's parents, friends, and business associates, who all chipped in enough to cover the lost £3000.

They played a handful of gigs, spread over a fortnight, including one to an audience of just nine people at the Hope and Anchor pub in Islington. It was a disaster. The Edge was

LEFT AND RIGHT: **Still hamming it up for the cameras . . . shrewd publicity stunts and clever marketing ensured that their first single *Out of Control* topped the Irish charts in September 1978. But they were still broke, and after a lukewarm reception to their first gigs in London McGuinness staged one of his most audacious stunts yet booking his unsigned 'baby band' for a gig at Dublin's 2000-capacity National Boxing Stadium.**

BELOW RIGHT: **Whatever the frustrations of finding a recording contract the band remained confident of their ability to triumph on stage. 'I knew we had something. I could feel the effect we had on the audience. The important thing was that we worked around that spark . . . fanning it' said Bono.**

struggling to play with a badly swollen hand, following a minor car accident with Adam in the rush to get to Dublin Airport. His fluidity was gone. Bono, meanwhile, assaulted his tiny audience with his usual manic flair. It was hopeless. They remained crushingly indifferent. The following night they opened as support for the all-girl group The Dolly Mixtures at the Rock Garden in Covent Garden. The gig was covered by *Melody Maker* but their reviewer mentioned not a word about U2. To add insult to injury they appeared in the *Melody Maker* gig guide as V2. Six days later, at the Canning Town Bridgehouse, they were billed as UR.

They returned to Dublin deflated. At yet another of what were beginning to seem like constant 'emergency' meetings McGuinness and his boys agonized about what to do. Financially they were at crisis point – they barely had enough to live on, let alone tour on. It was then that McGuinness's most audacious bluff crystallized. OK, so they were broke. But they could still act big-time. They would book up a major Irish

tour, climaxing in a gig to 2000 people at the National Boxing Stadium. For an unsigned band to headline there on the strength of winning five categories in a recent *Hot Press* poll was either foolhardy or arrogant. But McGuinness was convinced they could pull it off. He even used the gig to entice the next record company bigwig on his list, Island A & R man Bill Stewart. To coincide with the tour they would also release their second single, *Another Day*.

Three other Island executives, from the company's publishing wing, Blue Mountain, were persuaded to see the band perform at Queen's University in Belfast. The tour had been going well and, although some audiences could be tough, Bono had never encountered a wall of abuse of the kind he and the others received that night. 'Stop fucking preaching and play, you can't fucking play,' screamed one heckler. It was one of the lowest points in their fledgling careers. There was nothing to do but go back to Dublin and pin their tattered hopes on the Boxing Stadium. Tickets were

going slowly. Fewer than 500 had been sold. They made up numbers with a guest list. Family, friends, people who were only on a nodding acquaintance with Bono or Adam were invited. The audacious bluff was a brilliant victory. Queen's and Belfast were far behind them as they rode the wave of affection emanating from these Dubliners.

In later years Bill Stewart from Island was to recall: 'One biting cold night in February 1980 a shivering talent-spotter found himself in Dublin on what was beginning to look like another wild goose chase. The evidence of a pretty dire single and the urgings of a persistent but, as yet, unproven manager did little to lift my spirits. Suddenly, in a burst of white light, four slight figures pounced on stage, picked up their instruments as if they were soldiers seizing weapons and tore into their first song with a deafening roar. It was electrifying. It was the first night I saw U2.'

Suitably dazzled Stewart flew back to London to talk to Island boss Chris Blackwell. Blackwell was uncertain and wanted instead to sign Spandau Ballet, a clean-cut group of Londoners at the vanguard of the New Romantics movement. They argued all afternoon but eventually Stewart convinced Blackwell that turning down U2 would make him look as foolish as those record company executives who had first turned down The Beatles . . .

The link-up with Island was the first serious breakthrough for U2. The label's musical integrity was renowned. Blackwell had made his fortune by signing a little-known Jamaican reggae artist called Bob Marley. In the late Sixties Island turned its attentions to rock music. By the end of the Seventies the label had released albums by an impressive stable of musicians – Traffic, Free, King Crimson, Mott The Hoople, Fairport Convention, Emerson, Lake and Palmer, and Roxy Music. With the arrival of punk Blackwell had nurtured such signings as Ultravox and Eddie and the Hot Rods.

The deal guaranteed them £50,000 upfront, four albums using original material which Island would accept unseen, and a further £50,000 to fund international tours.

They had three months before beginning to record their debut album at Dublin's Windmill Studios which was to become virtually their home from home in later years. Meanwhile they were to set out on a long British tour to establish a market for their album and to promote their first Island single, *11 O'clock, Tick Tock*; this was produced by Martin Hamnett, the man behind respected and individual British bands like Joy Division and The Teardrop Explodes. The single still did not chart in the UK. A hymn to disaffected youth – 'We thought we had the answers, it was the questions we had wrong' – its dark, cavernous, aural landscape featuring a white-noise snare and guitars that were not so much metallic as rusty reflected more about Hamnett than it did about the still-crystallizing U2.

Response to their live performances was encouraging however. Though *Melody Maker* had effectively ignored their previous gigs it now published an ecstatic review of their concert at the Hammersmith Clarendon. 'Easily the finest display of awe-inspiring rock that I've witnessed in a long time. It contained just about every emotion . . . from anger to savagery, beauty and that indefinable essence where mere words become useless,' wrote reviewer Paolo Hewitt.

And later Ian Pye, also from *Melody Maker*, was to say: 'U2 should establish themselves as one of the best things to come out of Ireland since James Joyce and Guinness.'

The Shalom prayer group had become increasingly important to Larry, The Edge, and Bono. They had willingly accepted its doctrine that 'unless you be born again by water and the spirit you shall not see the Kingdom of Heaven.' They had been baptized by immersion in the sea, and, when possible, attended the prayer meetings twice a week. Bono, particularly, had changed. He stopped mooning and chasing girls. Instead he was committed to Ali, the girl he would later marry and with whom he had been smitten since Mount Temple. The Edge was also going steady with his future wife, Aislinn. Larry, too, had a stable relationship with a girl called

11 O'CLOCK TICK TOCK

Ann. That left only Adam . . .

He had attended an early meeting but had decided it just wasn't for him. He was too busy enjoying the rock'n'roll lifestyle, as far as was possible for a bass guitarist little heard of outside Dublin.

Their brief connexion with Martin Hamnett ended when he was unable to produce their next single because of the tragic suicide of the lead singer of Joy Division, the group with which he was most closely associated. Instead Blackwell suggested Steve Lillywhite who had enjoyed conspicuous success with many Island signings and other contemporary artists like Ultravox, Toyah, XTC, and Peter Gabriel. The single, again produced at Windmill, was a so-so song about teenage suicide called *A Day Without Me*.

Lillywhite hated the single but loved U2. It was agreed that he would produce their debut album, *Boy*, which featured 12 songs that were ample testimony to the essence of the band and the extent to which it had grown and developed since those early sessions in Larry Mullen's kitchen. The critical reception was fantastic. Lyndon Barber, of *Melody Maker*, said: 'U2's live performances have raised their audience's expectations to what must have seemed like an impossible height, but not only have they reached that peak with their first album, they've risen above it.' Other reviewers said it was among the finest debut albums of all time – joining an elite company which in every poll includes artists like Roxy Music, The Velvet Underground, Patti Smith, and The Rolling Stones. One American rock writer said the album was the first to affect him as much as The Who's *My Generation*.

This last quote must have pleased Bono greatly. Just before the release of *Boy* in November 1980 he told reporters:

LEFT: After signing with Island U2 embarked on a long British tour. An early review described their performance as 'Easily the finest display of awe-inspiring rock that I have witnessed in a long time.' Next would come Europe and America.

'Even from the very start we wanted something like the sensitivity of, say, Neil Young, with the power of The Who.'

The album opened with *I Will Follow*, which became the band's third Island single in Britain and the first in America. Opening with The Edge's jangling guitar, closely followed by a thunderous drum roll, *I Will Follow* exploded like an atom bomb and continued, like a roller coaster of raw energy right through to the closing track, an old-time favorite, *Shadows and Tall Trees*.

There was an unexpected and silly furore surrounding the album's cover shot which featured a young boy naked from the waist up. The pose, which some felt was reminiscent of a cheesecake centerfold, prompted a child-pornography scandal. The accusations were strongly denied by the shocked band, but it forced them to commission a redesign of the cover for the American market. No publicity is bad publicity, of course, and the fuss did arouse interest in the album – though not enough to push it to the higher echelons of the charts in either Britain or America. It rested at #2 in Britain and #4 in the US. The top of the charts were still dominated by performers like Barbra Streisand, Abba, Barry Manilow, George Benson, and Johnny Mathis.

Bono put words to their disappointment. 'Nice is a horrible word . . . music for lifts, music for supermarkets.

ABOVE: *Melody Maker* predicted that U2 would establish themselves 'as one of the best things to come out of Ireland since James Joyce and Guinness.'

INSET LEFT: Adam seemed to be increasingly isolated as the only non-Christian member of the band.

That's fine if you're going up and down, but I want more than that out of music' and, 'I can tell when a singer is singing what's in his heart. There's lots of glossy pop songs that can maybe make us cry, but it's a bit like watching *Little House On The Prairie*.'

Paul McGuinness was more optimistic. Even before *Boy* was released he had been talking to Chris Blackwell at Island about putting U2 on the road in America. Blackwell had suggested he contact Frank Barsalona, a tough-talking, no-nonsense Italian-American whose New York-based Premier Talent agency, while not the biggest agency in the States was certainly one of the most prestigious. Barsalona was the man behind some of the biggest stadium-status acts in the world, acts like The Who and Bruce Springsteen.

The two had met in fall 1980, just before *Boy* was released in the States. They hit it off immediately. Maybe it was just the kind of sixth sense that you get from 20 years in the rock'n'roll business but Barsalona had a hunch that the four Dublin boys could make it, and make it BIG.

Why not bring them out for a short 10-day East Coast tour in December and then a major three-month assault in spring 1981? Great, said McGuinness.

They would start at the bottom. Barsalona lined up a debut gig at the Penny Arcade in Rochester, New York. It was a million miles from Madison Square Garden, but it was a start. They would begin in the suburbs before playing in New York proper and moving on to other East Coast venues, notably in Boston, America's premier Irish city.

As luck would have it the Penny Arcade gig fell through and so U2 made their US debut in the most daunting of venues, a small New York ballroom called The Ritz. The date was 5 December 1980, three days before one of their biggest heroes, John Lennon, was gunned down as he signed autographs for a madman outside his New York home, the Dakota Building.

The venue was far from ideal. Barsalona recalled: 'You usually book a week or 10 days outside of New York and work your way in.' The Rochester cancellation left him no choice but to debut his new band in New York before they had had a chance to work their set in. Worse, as he added: 'The Ritz usually had dance bands every Friday, Saturday and Sunday night and they filled the place up with people who wanted to dance. I knew the place would be packed, but not with people who wanted to see U2.'

Full of trepidation Barsalona took his seat, along with a small group of guests, mainly executives from Warner Brothers, who he had invited along to see 'this great new band from Ireland'. The audience wasn't so much hostile as indifferent. Ten minutes or so into the set Bono stopped the band. Memories of Queen's University in Belfast loomed large in Paul McGuinness's mind. 'We're up here,' Bono was shouting to the crowds gathered around the bar. Then turning to Barsalona and his VIP guests he roared: 'We've come to play for you. Get off your fat arses and dance if you want to dance.' People started to notice, just one or two at first, but then more and more. The band gave them everything they had. 'With every song,' recalled Barsalona, 'a little part of the audience started paying attention. It was almost like a wave. When they were about 60% through they basically had the whole audience. I still get chills when I think about it.'

When the set was over, Frank Barsalona, one of the most important men in American rock music, ran to the

THESE PAGES: U2 began their assault on the US with a short East Coast tour in September 1980 followed by three months in Spring 1981. They started at the bottom playing a New York ballroom three days before John Lennon was murdered outside the Dakota building. The initial response was not so much hostile as indifferent but by the end of the set Frank Barsalona was persuaded. He promised them 'I give you my word. You are going to happen in America.'

dressing room and, carried away with emotion, pushed Bono, The Edge, Adam, and Larry into a corner and spluttered; 'I've got to tell you something . . . I know you've had a difficult time getting airplay. But I give you my word, you are going to happen in America.'

Much the same thing happened seven nights later at Boston's Paradise Theater where U2 took second billing to a rebel-rousing Detroit rock'n'roll band called Barooga. Perhaps it was because the local radio station, WBCN, had been heavily plugging their records, perhaps it was all down to their performance on the night but, at the end of it, there was no doubt which band was the main attraction. As soon as U2 left the stage the crowds started to flood out of the Paradise Theater in droves. Only a few stalwarts stayed to see Barooga.

In January 1981 U2 topped nine categories in the annual *Hot Press* poll. They spent most of the first two months touring in the UK, playing venues like London's Lyceum Ballroom (where 700 fans were locked out) and a prestigious residency at the famous Marquee Club. Money was tight; they drove around in a small van, staying at cheap hotels. Their only indulgence was to eat at restaurants recommended in *The Good Food Guide*. They also made their European debuts in Belgium and Holland.

In the spring they went back to America. This time,

THESE PAGES: In spring 1981 U2 returned to America traveling far and wide to cities like Dallas, Chicago (above), Los Angeles, Washington DC, San Francisco, and Seattle. America loved their energy and passion. But on long hours on the tour bus the tension was palpable. Rumor had it that Adam spent the journeys chatting to McGuinness at the front while at the back Bono, The Edge, and Larry sat reading The Bible.

however, they toured far and wide, venturing to places like Dallas, Chicago, Los Angeles, Washington DC, San Francisco, and Seattle.

America loved them, but they were beginning not to love themselves. The tension was palpable on the tour bus, mainly because of the divisions over Christianity. Adam was beginning to feel increasingly isolated. Rumors were rife that the other three weren't talking to him. Whether or not that was true it is a matter of record that he spent the journeys chatting

to McGuinness at the front of the bus while Bono, The Edge, and Larry sat at the back reading *The Bible*.

It was against this mixed background of triumph and conflict that U2 flew into Nassau on 22 April for a 10-day break. Producer Steve Lillywhite had joined them on the last leg of the American tour to familiarize himself with the new material they had been writing for their second album. While in Nassau the band joined the illustrious ranks of Talking Heads, the Tom Tom Club, and Robert Palmer in visiting the famous

Compass Point studios to lay down their next single, *Fire*.

Clever marketing again came to their aid. Island dreamed up the idea for a limited-edition double-pack single which would feature not just the regular A and B sides, but also a special live disc. The single provided U2 with their first major hit. *Fire* reached #5 in the British charts shortly after its release in June 1981.

That month, back at Windmill, the band began recording their second album, *October*. Though it has its fans,

it was far from the album they had been expected to deliver. After *Boy* Bono had, in a moment of extravagant enthusiasm, talked of making an epic album like The Beatles' *Sergeant Pepper's Lonely Hearts' Club Band*. Opinions vary but *October* was not that album – it revealed a band developing and perfecting their own unique sound, but somehow at the expense of content. The Edge's guitar was more restrained, Adam's bass more assured, Larry's drums were tighter and, where once Bono had cried to the skies, he was now more

THESE PAGES: **In June 1981 U2 had their first major hit with a track called *Fire* which reached #5 in Britain. When their second album, *October*, was finally released in November 1981 U2 had jetted off again for a 20-date coast-to-coast tour of America. The trip was not without its problems. On the eve of leaving Bono, The Edge, and Larry considered pulling out, feeling that they could not reconcile their Christian beliefs with being in a rock 'n' roll band. But commonsense prevailed, and they triumphed playing gigs to 3000-plus capacity crowds across the States. By their next US tour in early 1982 they were playing 10,000-15,000 stadiums supporting the J Geils Band.**

mournful, almost melancholic. Despite the reservations *October* yielded a single, *Gloria*, an all-guns-blazing epic which reached #5 in the British charts while the album itself climbed to #11.

In August, while waiting for *October* to be released, U2 had co-headlined a gig with Thin Lizzy at Ireland's Slane Castle. Whether Adam reminded Phil Lynott of that 6am telephone call all those months before is uncertain. What is certain is that, by now, as many people had turned out to see U2 as had come to see Thin Lizzy.

The album might have done better if U2 had been around to promote it but in November, just one month after its release, U2 were due to set off again on a 20-date coast-to-

coast tour of America. Just before leaving a crisis flared up. Bono, The Edge, and Larry told McGuinness that they had decided not to go, that they could not reconcile their Christian beliefs with being in a rock'n'roll band. Shrewdly McGuinness listened calmly, saying he respected their feelings, but pointing out how hard Barsalona had worked on their behalf, asking them to consider all the people whose efforts would be disregarded if they pulled out, reminding them that he had negotiated $100,000 in tour support money from Warner Brothers.

Disaster was averted. They agreed to go. Barsalona had lined up gigs in halls with a 3000-plus capacity crowd right across America, including the deep South and the mid-West.

On the 20th and 21st of December they returned briefly to play two sell-out gigs at the Lyceum in London.

Gill Pringle of *Record Mirror* wrote: 'Words fail me. Everyone is hugging each other as they stumble outside.' Midway through the gig the bouncers had slapped a fan who was getting a bit carried away. Then they punched him. Incensed, Larry threw down his drumsticks and jumped into the audience. Bono followed and, between them, they managed to pull the heavies off. Back on stage Bono grabbed the microphone and called for the Lyceum management and pointed to the worst-offending bouncer: 'I want this guy out of here before we sing another song – NOW.' In January they toured Ireland where 10,000 fans saw them. 'U2 transformed this massive cowshed into an uninhibited exhibition of joy which has to be experienced to be believed,' wrote one reviewer of their gig at the massive, atmosphere-less Royal Dublin Society Hall.

In DJ Dave Fanning's poll of 50 All-Time Classics, U2 took six places, including the #1 slot for their single *11 O'clock, Tick Tock*.

They then returned for the second leg of their US tour, playing 10-15,000-seater stadiums as support for the J Geils Band, before returning for the summer to play festivals around Europe with headlining acts like The Eurythmics, Simple Minds and Peter Gabriel. They played just one gig in England, with The Police at Gateshead.

On 21 August 1982 Bono married Alison Stewart at the old Guinness Church of Ireland church in Raheny. He asked Adam to be his best man. It was a gesture of reconciliation, and an indication that the crisis had passed. Larry had decided to leave Shalom, The Edge was working on material for their third album, and a much more carefree Bono flew off on honeymoon to Jamaica.

In October the band released a new single – not an album track – called *A Celebration*. A raw, blistering song with a big Sixties' Who-like guitar, it peaked in the UK charts at #7. When Chris Blackwell had agreed to let his A & R man Bill Stewart sign U2 in March 1980 they had struck a wager. Blackwell had bet Stewart 100-1 against U2 having a #1 album inside three years. The deadline was drawing ominously near in January 1983 when the band released a single from the forthcoming album. The single, which is still one of their most popular tracks to date, was *New Year's Day*.

The album, *War*, which was to catapult them to megastardom, stormed into the #1 spot on the British album charts and the Top 10 in America almost as soon as it was released in March 1983.

'I think we've finally cracked it,' said Bono . . .

Even today *War*, which stayed in the charts for over a year, is remembered as one of the most commercially successful and creatively challenging albums of the Eighties.

Harsh and uncompromising, it marked a return to aggressive form for U2. As Bono explained: 'War seemed to be the motif for 1982. Everywhere you looked, from the Falklands to the Middle East to South Africa, there was war. By calling the new album *War*, we're giving people a slap in the face and, at the same time, getting away from the cosy image a lot of people have of U2.'

Some critics felt that without the signature 'Wall of Sound' created by The Edge and Larry that Bono's vocals sounded too exposed, too strained. Others noted that, although the band professed to be committed to peace, their style on this album and its title sounded worryingly militaristic. Bono, by now the unofficial spokesman for U2, had an answer for everybody. The feel was intentional, he said – they wanted to convey an atmosphere of the 'militant pacifism' of people they admired, like Martin Luther King.

The opening track, *Sunday, Bloody Sunday*, with its cascading violins, military drumming, and roared vocal, was a soaring giant of a song. U2 had always steered clear of writing about Northern Ireland and, as Bono now admitted: 'It was only going to America that made us think about Ireland.' Because U2 were Irish it was wrongly assumed, especially in the States, that they were pro-IRA. The song was indeed a reference to that fateful Sunday in 1972 when British paratroopers had mown down 13 unarmed people during a civil-rights march in Derry. But it could also be interpreted as a denouncement of the unyielding religions which tore Ireland apart, of the divisions which were echoed from the pulpit in churches across the land every Sunday.

The band had test-run the song at a concert in Belfast. Bono had told the audience that if they didn't like it U2 would never play it again. The song was not a rebel song but an emotional plea for love and sanity. 'Out of 3000 people in the hall only about three walked out. I think that says a lot about the audience's trust in us,' recalled The Edge.

Over an angry, jangling guitar introduction Bono sang:
'And the battle's just begun,
There's many lost, but tell me who has won?
The trenches dug within our hearts,
And mothers, children, brothers, sisters torn apart,
Sunday, Bloody Sunday'

While performing the song Bono would unfurl a huge white flag and pace the stage waving it. He had been depressed by the response of Americans to things like the Bobby Sands hunger strike. 'People were throwing money on to the stage and shouting for Bobby . . . I thought this guy

THIS MEANS WAR

must be so brave. But why? Why be so brave? Why die?' The flag was significant, he said, because 'As much as I would love to see a united Ireland I just don't believe you can put a gun to somebody's head to make him see your way. I was sick of the Green, White, and Orange, sick of the Stars and Stripes, sick of the Union Jack.'

Sunday, Bloody Sunday had been released as a single heralding the album in Europe (and later in the US) but was felt to be too inflammatory for release in Britain. Instead *New Year's Day*, a tribute to Poland's outlawed Solidarity movement, had been put out in January 1983. Little could the band have known when they were writing the song that the Polish authorities would lift the martial law imposed in the wake of the Solidarity riots on 1st January.

With the benefit of Island's creative marketing – releasing three different mixes of the song – *New Year's Day* became their biggest single to date, peaking in the UK at #10 and making it on to *Billboard*'s Top 100 in the States.

During the making of *War* a funny thing had happened to Bono as he waited at Heathrow Airport for a flight back to Dublin. He had bumped into Garrett Fitzgerald, leader of the Fine Gael party and shortly to become Prime Minister of Ireland. The two fell into an amiable argument about politics. Bono explained: 'I was asking him why politicians don't speak the language of the people, why they invented their own language which leaves the rest of the country out. I was saying that any leader of a country had to throw away the political language and speak to the people.' Fitzgerald, always one to spot a vote-catching idea, later contacted Bono and asked him to sit on an emergency committee on unemployment in Ireland.

Bono agreed. 'But I realized that I wasn't unemployed. I realized that I didn't want to speak at a committee meeting about rape without someone who had been raped being with

LEFT: 'I think we've finally cracked it' said Bono as the third album, *War*, went to # 1 in Britain.

me, didn't want to speak about unemployment without someone unemployed with me. I realized there was another language, committee-speak, and I didn't understand that. I didn't speak the language,' recalled Bono.

A second single from *War, Two Hearts Beat As One*, was released just after the album in March 1983. Despite the unrelenting backing of the Island publicity machine it struggled to peak at #18.

U2 had embarked on a 28-date promotional tour of

Britain in February, followed by a three-month tour of the US from April. U2's video for the *New Year's Day* single, a powerful testament to the horrors of war incorporating battle footage from the bloody German invasion of the Soviet Union during World War II, gained them crucial exposure on America's all-music TV channel, MTV.

On arrival Bono announced: 'We love playing in America. The audience reaction is instinctive. There isn't much reading on music. The only way people hear about things is by radio, which is very localised. You could be huge in Boston and people won't have heard of you in Texas.'

This time around U2 played almost exclusively at major festival sites or 10,000-seater football stadiums from North Carolina to Denver, from New York to Los Angeles. Bruce Springsteen came to see them play in Philadelphia. But the highlight of the tour was in June when U2 would headline the famous Red Rocks festival in Denver, Colorado.

Red Rocks is a spectacular configuration of sandstone bolders which jut out from the earth, making a natural amphitheater. McGuinness wanted to record and video the concert. His hopes were dampened considerably when the heavens opened just days before the concert and Denver endured its worst June weather this century. Nevertheless 8000 people braved the elements – their loyalty rewarded by

the sight of U2 on stage, a setting sun behind them, and the towering rocks silhouetted on the skyline. The resulting album (though sound was disappointing and some tracks had been grafted on from other concerts) was called *Under A Blood Red Sky* and produced by Jimmy Iovine. It was released in November 1983 at the rock-bottom price of $4.98/£2.99 to foil bootleggers and became one of the very few live albums to reach #1. For the video, fans had to wait till July 1984.

The only minus point to Red Rocks was that the band had to pay out $50,000 for Bono's impromptu rendition – without permission – of Stephen Sondheim's *Send in the Clowns*.

High on Red Rocks the band moved into the last leg of their US tour. Unease had been growing for weeks about Bono's nightly, and sometimes risky, forays into the audience.

Typically, a few bars into the surging *Boy* track, *The Electric Co* (written about a friend of Bono's who was given electric shock treatment in a Dublin mental hospital), he would be off – climbing up scaffolding beside the stage, clambering into the balconies, anything to attract attention. He never knew where he was going or what was going to happen, but he was driven by some manic desire to make contact with the audience. One night the microphone cable had wrapped around his neck, almost choking him. Seemingly oblivious to warnings that these stunts were dangerous, that he was inciting hysteria, that he would hurt himself or somebody else, Bono was up to his old tricks again when the band took to the stage of the Los Angeles Sports Stadium on 17 June.

The Edge's frenetic guitar announced the song and, suddenly, Bono was off again – up the stairs behind the stage,

LEFT: In spring 1983 U2 embarked on another huge tour of the States playing almost exclusively major festival sites or football stadiums. The highlight came in June when they headlined the legendary Red Rocks Festival in Denver, Colorado. The concert, when 8000 people braved freak weather conditions, was captured on video and led to the live album, *Under a Blood Red Sky*. The only down side was that they had to pay heavily for Bono's impromptu rendition of Sondheim's *Send in the Clowns*. He caused a near riot too in Los Angeles.

RIGHT: A taste of things to come . . . at the end of the *War* tour the band donated their backdrop to a museum which was exhibiting paintings by survivors of the Atomic bombs at Hiroshima and Nagasaki. The title was *The Unforgettable Fire*.

around the balcony, white flag in one hand, radio microphone in the other, his sound technician desperately trying to keep up. He was almost opposite the stage when a fight broke out in front of him and somebody grabbed the flag. Bono stood on the rim of the balcony and threatened to jump if it didn't stop. It didn't and, apparently omnipotent now, Bono jumped 20 feet to be caught by the audience below. The sound technician followed, so did others. Madness had erupted, the flag was ripped, hands clutched at him. Frightened, Bono lashed out wildly. Someone hit back. He had gone too far . . .

In the dressing room afterwards the anger exploded. 'The boys took me aside backstage and said "Look, cut it out. You're the singer in a band, you've just got to get up there and sing. You don't have to remind the audience that U2 aren't stars to be worshipped – they already understand,"' recalled a suitably chastened Bono.

At the end of this tour U2 donated their *War* backdrop and stage set to the Chicago Peace Museum where it was exhibited alongside a series of paintings by Japanese survivors of the atomic bombs at Hiroshima and Nagasaki. The collection was titled *The Unforgettable Fire*.

The band returned to Dublin to headline *A Day at the Races*, a day-long event before 25,000 people in Dublin's Phoenix Park. Also on the bill were Simple Minds, The Eurythmics, and Big Country.

For the remainder of 1983 and the early part of 1984 the band were preoccupied with writing material for their new album. They were hungry for a change of direction, a new challenge. There was only one man they wanted to produce it – Brian Eno. It was an unlikely alliance. While U2 were rootsy, passionate performers, Eno had made his name as the electronics wizard who played synthesizer to archetypal smoothies Roxy Music. His solo albums since had titles like *Music for Films, Music for Airports, Discreet Music*. He had collaborated successfully as a producer with David Bowie and Talking Heads' singer David Byrne.

When first approached he turned them down flat. Recalled Eno: 'However, they just kept nagging me, so much so that I listened to some of their old material, which didn't inspire me particularly. But I was mystified by their reasons for wanting me. Once I'd met Bono I knew I had to work with him. There was something about him. He talked about the band in a way that I hadn't heard anyone doing in a long while and so, on that basis, out of curiosity I agreed to work with them.' Bono himself said Eno was attracted because he had been living on a constant diet of black gospel music and could feel the parallels with the intensity of U2.

In March 1984 *Rolling Stone* magazine in America chose U2 as its Band of the Year for the *War* tour in 1983. The

timing was perfect for Paul McGuinness who was negotiating a better deal with Island. For the next four albums U2 would receive $2 million an album and double the royalties, they could choose the producer and Island would accept all album material unheard, and each album would be promoted by three videos at a cost of $75,000 each, paid for by Island. Finally, perhaps the biggest coup of all, U2 would get all their publishing rights back. The deal effectively set them up for life. Bono, The Edge, Adam, and Larry were multi-millionaires. And

the oldest of them was still only 24.

After months holed away with Brian Eno and his assistant Danny Lanois in Slane Castle, a 200-year-old stone fortress about 30 miles outside Dublin, the band finally began recording at Windmill Studios.

Perhaps because they recognized how much hung on this album U2 kept over-running the deadlines and booking more studio time. They were due to tour Australia in September and they were cutting things a bit fine. They finally

INSET AND BELOW: Bono, by now a millionaire, still as hungry for adulation as in those early days in the pubs and clubs of Dublin.

handed the tapes to Island in August.

During August Bono still found time to accept an invitation to duet with Bob Dylan during the maestro's concert at Slane Castle. Dylan asked him if he knew *Blowin' in the Wind*. Bono nodded, but when it came to it he improvised with his own lyrics about barbed wire, soldiers, and Northern Ireland. Dylan was astonished, the crowd roared its approval. Bono had stuck to the spirit, if not the letter, of the song brilliantly. The gig forged a lasting friendship between the young man now being hailed as the savior of the Eighties and the man once hailed as the savior of the Sixties.

In September *Pride (In the Name of Love)* was released as a single in advance of the album, to be released in October. It was the clarion call that brought them thundering back into the charts. 'It is the most successful pop song we've ever written. I use the word pop in the best possible sense. Pop for me is an easily understood thing, you relate to it instinctively,' said Bono.

Pride was indeed U2 at their most anthemic, it was an unbridled, defiant, impassioned tribute to Martin Luther King. They hoped it would be the #1 they'd be waiting for but it peaked at #3 in the UK and didn't even make the US Top Ten.

The album, *The Unforgettable Fire* (the title was taken from the exhibition at the Chicago Peace Museum), did rather better, going straight to #1 in Britain. *Under a Blood Red Sky* was still at #30, *War* was at 41 and *October* had only just dropped out from #94. In America it reached the Top 10 just

ABOVE: *The Unforgettable Fire* album was their most successful yet. Bono said that *Pride (In the Name of Love)* was the best 'pop' song they'd ever written. It was a tribute to Martin Luther King.

RIGHT: Bono's predictions were beginning to come true. He was now likening the chemistry of U2 to that of supergroups like the Rolling Stones, The Who, and The Beatles.

six weeks after entering the charts at #47.

Bono's ability to create on the run was ably demonstrated on *The Unforgettable Fire*. At one point in the recording Eno had handed Bono a microphone 'and told me to sing over this piece of music which had been slowed down, played backwards, whatever. So I did it and when it was finished there were all these beautiful lines and melodies coming out of it. I said I couldn't wait to finish it. Eno said "What do you mean, finish it? It is finished"' That track was *Elvis Presley and America*.

The album, their most accomplished yet, also featured *The 4th of July* and *Bad*, the song which was to seal their fortunes later on at Live Aid.

The second single from the album, the title track, made it to #6 in Britain the following April.

Way back in 1981 Bono had been happily telling music journalists: 'I feel that we are meant to be one of the great groups. There's a certain chemistry about The Stones, The Who and The Beatles and I think it's also special about U2.' Albums success was one thing and, though five years later he still did not admit to any doubts, privately he was despondent that U2 had yet to have a single at #1 . . .

U2 flew out on their biggest tour yet in the autumn of 1984, which would take them to Australia, New Zealand, Germany, Italy, France, Belgium, Holland, Switzerland, America, Britain, and back to Ireland. They had delivered *The Unforgettable Fire* so late that they barely had time to rehearse, and quickly discovered that they could not reproduce on stage the orchestral feel created with Eno at Windmill Studios.

Australia was a disappointment – the band were unhappy with their performances despite playing to capacity crowds. At one 12,000-seater concert fighting broke out in the crowd. Bono again stopped the music and, pointing an accusing finger at the audience, roared: 'We do not have violence at U2 gigs. Not ever. Enough.'

Next came New Zealand, with similarly mixed results, where the band added a young Maori named Greg Carroll to their entourage. He was to be a kind of glorified 'gofer,' with special responsibilities to (and for) Bono.

From there they went to Europe. It was mayhem . . . for one gig they came out playing *Gloria* in two different keys. The Edge blamed it on Adam who 'didn't notice because he's tone deaf'; in Paris they played in a large tent set in the decaying industrial heartlands where the movie *Diva* was filmed; in Brussels the band's amplification set off an earthquake alarm at the nearby Belgium Royal Observatory. Again they blamed it on Adam.

The British dates opened with two nights at London's Brixton Academy before moving on to gigs in Glasgow, Edinburgh, Birmingham, and Manchester. They then returned for two nights at the Wembley Arena before heading home to Dublin for a quick break before setting off for a handful of pre-Christmas shows in the States as a prelude to a four-month US tour from February 1985.

Just before leaving for the first leg in America Bono and Adam returned to London to pledge their support for Bob Geldof's Band Air project. They joined the elite gathering of stars, including Sting, George Michael, Midge Ure, Paul Weller, Spandau Ballet, Paul Young, and Boy George, who gathered together on that bleak November Sunday to record *Do They Know It's Christmas?/Feed the World* to raise money for famine relief in Ethiopia.

As soon as U2 touched down in New York a few days before its 10-date December tour opener in Philadelphia the band members realized just how dramatically their popularity had soared in America. Their Manhattan hotel was under siege and, holed up in his room, Bono agreed to give a telephone interview to the Boston-based WBCN radio station which had been especially supportive since the early days. He finished on a pensive note: 'I'm on the 22nd floor of the Parker Meridien

AN UNFORGETTABLE FIRE

hotel, there's a lot of people downstairs, I can't walk out on the street because people are pushing up against us. So, as I say, I'm on the 22nd floor, in this hotel room, and I wish I was on stage. I don't like this waiting around.' Within moments the frantic hotel manager was on the line to their room, complaining that the hotel switchboard was hopelessly jammed. Bono realized that, without thinking, he had given the hotel name out during the interview and could barely believe that the Meridien was now under a massive long-distance assault from Boston.

Everywhere they went they were feted. Exhausted, but triumphant, they returned home to Dublin for Christmas and the New Year before flying back to the States in February 1985.

This time they were playing only major stadiums. Bono, who always craved contact with the audience, accepted that, in the interests of safety, it was plain stupid to go running off the stage on a whim. But it was still routine for stray fans to beat the security, scale the barriers, and climb on stage. Bono usually dealt with this by slow dancing with the girls, or embracing the men. In Los Angeles again one night he discovered there was potential for even this simple act to become more threatening. A young man bolted up and clasped the singer in a tight bear hug. Bono motioned to the stage assistants to help and finally, after a very long 30 seconds, kneeled down on the floor and rolled over to break the youth's grasp. In Detroit he was incensed when somebody threw an Irish tricolor on stage. 'Stop fighting! Don't you know that's what the problem is all about,' bellowed Bono.

The outspoken singer was also the target of death threats. In Los Angeles someone sent a gun license to U2's offices and police thought someone had gotten into the gig with a gun. At one point there were almost more security men around than fans. 'I just laughed it off. It was like the *Blues*

LEFT: Bono relaxing after Live Aid.

Brothers – "We're on a mission from God and we ain't finished yet!" said Bono.

Live performances of *The Unforgettable Fire* material had finally come together. Now Bono was having fun. He would drop refrains of other artists' material in – songs like *Ruby Tuesday*, Lou Reed's *Waiting for my Man, Amazing Grace, Send in the Clowns, Knockin' on Heaven's Door* . . . For eight weeks U2 traveled the length and breadth of America, although they were now traveling in a hired four-engine Vickers Viscount.

In March *Rolling Stone* magazine named U2 as 'Our Choice: Band of the Eighties.'

With their latest album a platinum success and four of their five albums on the *Billboard* Top 200 chart, U2 were kings of all they surveyed when they walked on stage at Madison Square Garden on 1st April. In another stroke of genius McGuinness had flown a party of British and Irish journalists over to see the show. He wanted to ensure that they were the hottest ticket in town when they finally returned to the UK and Ireland.

In front of families and friends, as well as 16,000 fans, they were swept away on a wave of passion and energy.

Backstage afterwards Bono was heard to whisper: 'For an Irishman to be standing on that stage just means so much, not just for us, but for all Irishmen.'

They had played to half a million people by the time they played their final gig in Florida on 4 May. They had been on the road for eight solid months. Bono likened it to being a terrorist under interrogation in Northern Ireland. 'They put brown paper bags over their heads, they put them in rooms where they can't stand up or sit down with their legs stretched out, they keep the light on 24 hours a day so they don't know whether it's night or day. When you're on the road you can sometimes lose track of yourself. You become lost in time and space. You walk on stage, you give of yourself for an hour and a half and the applause that comes back is uplifting, but sometimes it's anonymous. You end up going back to this empty space which is your hotel room. It's a bit like the guy with the paper bag over his head.'

U2 returned to Ireland as heroes. Thanks to the pre-publicity from the New York stunt, tickets for their homecoming gig, at Croke Park, were going well. On the night 55,000 turned out to welcome home the four young men who had put the pride back in Dublin.

Just two weeks later and they made their memorable appearance at Live Aid. By now U2 were being hailed as the undisputed saviors of rock – everybody wanted a piece of them. Two months after Live Aid Bono was invited to listen in

ABOVE LEFT: The Edge and Bono during the 1984 *Unforgettable Fire* tour, at a memorable gig in Glasgow.

ABOVE: Bono with Sting. They were to work together at Live Aid and the 1986 Conspiracy of Hope tour for Amnesty International.

ABOVE RIGHT: Bono in France.

LEFT: The quiet man of rock, The Edge, wearing his trademark trilby hat.

RIGHT: Bono relaxing offstage at the 'Live Aid' concert.

THESE PAGES: U2 were happy to interrupt their punishing schedule in June 1986 to join Sting, Peter Gabriel, Joan Baez, Bryan Adams, the Neville Brothers, Jackson Browne, and Lou Reed on the Conspiracy of Hope tour to celebrate Amnesty International's 50th anniversary. The tour earned Amnesty $4million and tripled its membership in the States. The cause is still very dear to their hearts – they later urged fans to join and support Amnesty on the cover notes of their album *Achtung Baby*.

on Keith Richards and Mick Jagger jamming in a New York recording studio. After joining in with them he was asked to sing something of his own. Embarrassed that he had nothing new in mind Bono retreated to his hotel room and wrote *Silver and Gold*, about South Africa.

His admiration for his teenage idol Keith Richards was fulsome. 'He is a man with all the infamy and fortune anyone could want and it all means very little to him. The music is the all-important thing. He hasn't taken the bait and been middle-classed out like so many others. When he straps on a guitar all the lines on his face just disappear.'

In November 1985 the band cloistered themselves away in Larry's new seaside home in the Dublin suburb of Howth and began working on the new album. The pressure on them was intense. So overwhelmed were they by it that they didn't actually deliver the album, again produced by Eno and Lanois, until March 1987.

They were ordered to keep a low profile in this period and concentrate on the album. Larry never gave interviews anyway, The Edge was more into the music, Adam was into the rock-star lifestyle; and Bono, well, at times it had seemed as though Bono was secretly delighted to play the media darling and cast himself in the role of rock Messiah.

Just before Christmas, however, Bono did find time to go into the studio to record with his old friends, the Donegal-based Irish band Clannad. The band were perhaps best known for writing and singing the mournful and melodic theme to the British TV series *Harry's Game*. In much the same mold the single, *In a Lifetime*, featured Bono duetting with Clannad's female lead, Maire Ni Bhraonain.

In June 1986 U2 interrupted their recording to go back on the road for one week to fulfil a promise they had made to Amnesty International. On the Conspiracy of Hope tour, U2 headlined with Sting, Peter Gabriel, Joan Baez, Bryan Adams, the Neville Brothers, Jackson Browne, and Lou Reed. The tour earned Amnesty $4 million and tripled its membership in the States.

When *The Joshua Tree* was released it made shock

waves, catapulting them to the crest of superstardom. The title came from the name of a tree capable of flourishing even in the most sun-scorched desert, a metaphor for U2's ability to survive and conquer the turbulent world of rock megastardom. It was dedicated to Greg Carroll, the young, cheerful Maori roadie they had picked up in New Zealand but who had been killed in a road accident while running an errand for Bono in Dublin.

Record shops in Belfast and London opened at midnight on the day of the release of *The Joshua Tree*. Within a week of its release it had sold 300,000 copies – a feat not accomplished since the Beatles *For Sale* album – and it crashed into the album charts at #1. Where *The Unforgettable Fire* had sold six million worldwide, *The Joshua Tree* would go

on to top 14 million. It was a return to the rootsiness of early U2 but with so much depth in several ways: more maturity than *Boy*, more poetry than *October* and more coherence than *The Unforgettable Fire*.

It yielded three singles – their first real love song, *With or Without You* which reached #4 in Britain, *I Still Haven't Found What I'm Looking For* in May (#6) and *Where the Streets Have No Name* in August (#4).

U2 had got the success they craved, they became the first British band since The Who to be given the cover of *Time* magazine. They had the whole world at their feet, but they still hadn't found what they were looking for. What they wanted, what they needed to ensure their place among the élite of rock, was a single that would get to #1 . . .

In the aftermath of *The Joshua Tree* it began to look as if Bruce Springsteen was yesterday's pan-global thing. Paul McGuinness couldn't get over his luck in finding them that lackluster night in May 1978.

He would shake his head and laugh as he told journalists: 'When I first met them they could hardly play a note, but I always knew they'd be big some day. We'd spend hours discussing how we would take over the world.' And take over the world was exactly what they seemed to have done in the summer and fall months of 1987.

Bono said it was 'amazing' to think of people in Dublin picking up *Time* magazine and seeing an Irish band on the cover. 'For so long we were thought of as a British band and that was insulting. To be covered by the international media finally means we've been accepted as Irish.'

Universally they were hailed as the torch-bearers of rock 'n' roll. On the cover of every kind of magazine, the 'U2 phenomenon' analyzed in newspaper editorials. Garrett Fitzgerald said they were 'an inspiration to Ireland,' the Press deified Bono as a the ultimate rock icon – a cross between the Morrisons, Jim and Van.

Bono, still only 27, turned it all into a joke in an attempt to stop it going to his head. 'When we played in the States college professors came down to do a thesis on The Edge's guitar sound . . . other people like U2 because they think Larry's James Dean, or they think I'm John Paul II.'

Larry himself was more straightforward: 'It's not bad, is it, for a bunch of yobbos from north Dublin.'

The album, though less of a concept album than *War* or *The Unforgettable Fire*, contained some of their most accomplished work. Bono, who had suffered constant anxiety about his abilities as a vocalist, suddenly found the power and the emotion to match The Edge's guitar on *Bullet the Blue Sky* – a searing Led Zeppelin-like track condemning American imperialism in El Salvador and Nicaragua.

Where the Streets Have no Name was an unpretentious, solid rock song, while *With or Without You* their most successful attempt yet at a poignant love song; *In God's Country* and *Trip Through Your Wires* exposed the country influences to which they had succumbed while touring extensively in the States; *Red Hill Mining Town* was a bona-fide anthem, *One Tree Hill* a somber, beautiful elegy to Greg Carroll; and *The Mothers of the Disappeared* a reverent tribute to the long-suffering women of Argentina.

That last track was inspired by Bono's trip to Central America. He explained: 'After doing the Amnesty tour I started on this trail. I didn't want to go there but then I decided to. If you're the subject of the media you don't trust the media. I went with Lou Reed to visit Chilean refugees and graffiti artists

THE JOSHUA TREE

in the Latin Quarter of San Francisco and ended up in Nicaragua.' Nicaragua, he said, was 'the sexiest revolution you ever saw. Women in khaki uniforms standing on corners with Armalite rifles. They were standing there smoking cigarettes but looking like Miss World.'

Finally Bono had often talked of his dream of writing one truly classic song . . . and he had done it on the passionate and powerful *Still Haven't Found What I'm Looking For.* 'I don't know where it came from. It's as if it's always been written. It was just plucked out of the air . . .' said Bono.

Far from resting on their laurels U2 set off on the road again, to undertake their biggest world tour yet. It would be a full year before they returned home again, and the tour would take them across the world, playing 110 dates to three million people, and gross them at least $35 million.

The tour got off to a bad start when the plane carrying them to America was struck by lightning, temporarily knocking out the lights and the radar. Sophia Loren was a fellow passenger. Terrified, she cowered in her seat and was only comforted when Bono leaned over and said to her: 'God must have been taking a picture of you.' Well, what do you expect? He's Irish, he must have kissed the Blarney Stone.

In the US Bono was accident prone. His voice failed him in Arizona, forcing the band for the first time ever to cancel; another night he fell and gashed his chin; at yet another concert he fell foul of the authorities when he was held to have created a fire risk when he invited the fans to 'come on down.' A road manager had to offer himself for arrest because he'd signed a form accepting responsibility for 'civil disturbances.' In the end no charges were brought but the incident only served to remind everyone that they still had a bit of a loose cannon in Bono.

LEFT: **By 1987 all the initial problems of integration and confidence were a thing of the past for Adam Clayton.**

47

LEFT: Larry Mullen, one member of the band who resisted rather than courted publicity. No matter how he tried, however, he was unable to get away from his tag as the pinup boy, James Dean lookalike of U2.

BELOW: In the aftermath of *The Joshua Tree* The Edge's inspired guitar playing drew even college professors keen to do a thesis on his technique. The comparisons just grew and grew, from Hendrix to Clapton to Led Zeppelin's Jimmy Page.

RIGHT: Bono had always dreamed of writing one truly epic song, and felt he had done it with the passionate Gospel-inspired *I Still Haven't Found What I'm Looking For.* 'I don't know where it came from. It's as if it's always been written. It was just plucked out of the air,' he said. Critics now described him as a cross between Morrisons, Van and Jim.

The Edge had once said that U2 'were the worst covers band in the world. That's why we had to start writing our own material!' Yet now they were working endless covers into their live shows – the Dylan classic *Maggie's Farm* (Dylan actually joined them on stage for a Los Angeles gig, singing *Knockin' on Heaven's Door*), *Sympathy for the Devil* by The Stones, *Riders on the Storm* by The Doors, *Helter Skelter* and *Cold Turkey* by John Lennon, *People Get Ready* by Curtis Mayfield, *Love Will Tear Us Apart*, a pessimistic modern classic by British band Joy Division.

Traveling in the States they had started exploring rock's back catalog. Bono, particularly, was overwhelmed by the power of blues and gospel music. There were, he felt, undeniable links with Irish music. Doing so many covers simply reflected his delight with this musical journey. 'I was 25 when I heard my first John Lee Hooker record, then I sat down and wrote *Silver and Gold.*'

Midway through the year they got a heroes' welcome when they played two 'homecoming' gigs in Dublin. *Time* magazine had called them 'the hottest ticket in rock' – and so it seemed as 100,000 people filed through the turnstiles to see them play at Croke Park.

Another epic event in Dublin turned sour. They had agreed to take part in Self Aid, aimed at raising money to help

Ireland's unemployed youngsters help themselves to find jobs. The politics behind the concert attracted criticism about the 'patronising' and 'condescending' politics of multi-millionaire rock stars. Though the bill boasted many big-name Irish stars, including Bob Geldof, Christy Moore, and Van Morrison, the vitriol seemed especially aimed at U2. This was hardly fair – though never inclined to trumpet their altruism U2 had invested greatly in Ireland. They had resisted constant pressure to leave Dublin for London, Paris, or New York but had opted to stay

and pay their taxes. It was reported that the Inland Revenue had to employ two officials full-time just to sort through their massive earnings. The band had also donated considerable funds to an arts center aimed at helping Irish musicians and were rumored to have bought around fifty businesses to improve employment possibilities for teenagers in Dublin.

U2 had crashed into 1987 unable to put a foot wrong, but by the end of the year the first worrying signs of a backlash were showing, at least in both the British and American Press.

LEFT: **Larry Mullen: the relentless touring pace of the band was beginning to take its toll on his wrists while (BELOW) Bono was beginning to suffer the sharp edge of the press's collective tongue. 'I talk too much' he admitted, but now he was even the victim of TV puppet satirists Spitting Image who sniped 'Bono thinks he's Jesus.'**

As The Edge commented: 'This year's been a dangerous year for U2. We're a household name, like Skippy Peanut Butter or Bailey's Irish Cream, and I suppose that makes us public property in a way we weren't before. We've seen the beginning of the U2 myth, and that can become difficult. Like, for instance, Bono's personality is now so caricatured that I worry whether he'll be allowed to develop as a lyricist the way I know he can,' he told *Rolling Stone*.

Bono was indeed becoming a victim of parody and

53

derision. Though admitting light-heartedly 'I talk too much' he just couldn't seem to stop. He had a view on religion, was scathing about the sex and drugs and rock'n'roll cliché, took up causes the way some people take up hobbies. Whether it was global warming, deforestation, world hunger, or civil rights – journalists could always rely on a lecture from Bono. He was beginning to be described as egocentric, earnestly grandiose. British television's satirical puppet show, *Spitting Image*, even turned its attentions to Bono's 'holier than thou' image with jokes about Bono, God, and St Peter. Newspapers and magazines were starting to run articles under headings like 'Aren't you sick of U2?'

Nevertheless, the 1987 annual *Rolling Stone* poll saw Bruce Springsteen beaten for the first time in years for Artist of the Year. The honor went to U2, who also seized the awards for Best Album, Best Single (*With or Without You* – a #1 in the US), Best Band, Best Live Performance, Best Songwriter (Bono), Best Album Cover, even Sexiest Male (Bono). The magazine's critics also named U2 as Best Band.

In February 1988 U2 kept a promise to Amnesty to play one concert in London to celebrate the human rights' organization's 40th anniversary. They had to decline the invitation to join Peter Gabriel on a tour that would take in China, Indonesia, Africa, the Soviet Union, and Latin America

LEFT AND FOLLOWING PAGES: In 1987 *Rolling Stone* readers voted Bono Best Songwriter and even Sexiest Man.

ABOVE: The band were voted Best Band and in 1988 *The Joshua Tree* won the Grammy for Album of the Year. By now they were being wooed as honored guests on America's celebrity circuit and (above) Bono arrives for a party at Jane Fonda's house in Hollywood.

because they were due in Los Angeles to finish editing their new double album and video, due to be released in October.

In March 1988 they won two Grammys, for Best Rock Performance By A Group, and Album Of The Year (*The Joshua Tree*). At the ceremony at New York's Radio City Music Hall Bono injected some humour by telling the 6000-strong audience: 'We'd like to thank Amnesty International, Desmond Tutu, Martin Luther King, Bob Dylan, Jimi Hendrix, Walt Disney, John the Baptist, George Best, Fawn Hall, Gregory

unimaginative, many of the newer tracks, like *Angel of Harlem* (a tribute to blues' singer Billie Holiday) and *When Love Comes to Town* (a duet with blues' maestro B B King) were 'self-indulgent,' and so on. Even the single, *Desire*, was said to sound more like Bo Diddley.

Film critics panned the film for its endless shots of Bono's armpits or band members piling into or emerging from limousines. What they seemed to fail to notice was that U2, the epitome of serious rock, were actually having fun. They

Peck, Doctor Ruth, Batman and Robin, Eddie the Eagle and, of course, Ronald Reagan.'

At the outset of their 1987 tour they had asked film-maker Phil Joanou to make a documentary which was eventually put on general release to coincide with the release of the album *Rattle and Hum*.

The sourness that had crept in at the end of that year had not gone away and both the album and film were savaged by the critics, who felt U2 had become complacent, regressive, and self-important. Their covers of classics like *Helter Skelter* and *All Along the Watchtower* were attacked for adding nothing new to the original, the inclusion of old favorites like *Pride, Bullet the Blue Sky* was said to be

were starstruck by meeting people like B B, they were entranced as they wandered tourist-like around Elvis's Graceland mansion, and who could deny the sheer joy on their faces as they watched a Harlem gospel choir transform *I Still Haven't Found What I'm Looking For*?

Needless to say the critics' mauling didn't hurt sales any. *Rattle and Hum* sold 11 million copies worldwide and went to the top of the album charts on both sides of the Atlantic. What's more, *Desire* provided them with that elusive British #1.

But the backlash was enough to shake their confidence so badly that they would not tour or release any material again until 1991.

LEFT: U2 at the Grammy Awards. Among those Bono thanked in his speech were Martin Luther King, Bob Dylan, Jimi Hendrix, Walt Disney, John the Baptist, George Best, Dr Ruth, Batman and Robin, and 'of course, Ronald Reagan.'

ABOVE: U2 during a break in filming *Rattle and Hum*.

RIGHT: Bono and The Edge perform *When Love Comes to Town* with BB King.

The lukewarm reception *Rattle and Hum* received in the States was not reflected in the rest of the world. Even in America *Rolling Stone* magazine's readers' poll in March 1989 saw them again win the Artist of the Year and Best Band, Best Album, Best Album Cover, Single *(Desire)*, Best Producer (Jimmy Iovine), Songwriter (Bono), Male Singer, Drummer, and Bassist. The Edge narrowly lost out as Best Guitarist to Van Halen. The band's hard-core following was as loyal as ever. But in the critics' poll there was no mention of U2.

They had returned to Britain in the winter of 1988 to promote the album. In one typical Press stunt the police had to stop them 'busking' to the crowds who had gathered to watch the celebrities arrive for the premiere of *Rattle and Hum* at the Empire cinema in London's Leicester Square.

In October Keith Richards had joined them on stage when they took part with Ziggy Marley, Robert Cray, and Womack and Womack for the Smile Jamaica benefit to raise thousands for the victims of Hurricane Gilbert. Early in 1989 the band won two more Grammys, for Best Rock Performance By A Group on *Desire* and Best Video Performance for *Where The Streets Have No Name*.

But for the remainder of the year controversy never seemed to be very far away. First came Adam's drugs bust. Just months after having a go at British and Irish customs men who always frisked him at airports because 'he's a musician, he must have drugs' and reiterating that the band were 'totally against drugs' Adam was found to be in possession of 19 grammes (¼ oz) of cannabis in a Dublin car park. He pleaded guilty to the charge and, in a deal permissable under Irish law, avoided a conviction by agreeing to pay £25,000 to a local charity. This was only weeks before U2 was about to embark on its next world tour which would take them to Australia, New Zealand, Europe – everywhere, in fact, except America.

The next controversy surrounded an official biography written by a leading Dublin sports writer, Eamon Dunphy. 'We intensely regret doing this book,' said Paul McGuinness. Allegations and counter allegations grabbed the tabloid headlines but Dunphy's book, *The Unforgettable Fire,* was still a bestseller and earned him a cool £250,000.

U2 finally came home from their tour to perform four shows in Dublin between Christmas and New Year at the newly opened Point Depot.

At the end of the last night Bono wound up the show saying: 'We've had a great 10 years, but we've got to do something else for a while . . . just to get away for a little while.' Speculation was rife that the band was splitting up for good. This was not the case, they stressed, they just needed a one-year break. 'Our brains are cluttered up. The strain of working has become unbearable. We need a break' said Bono.

THE U2 ZOO

He had hinted at the exhausting toll of constant touring in earlier interviews. Towards the end of 1987 he told journalists: 'When I was on the West Coast I was almost allergic to people for a while. . . . I was a commodity bought, sold and then redundant. It was like *Apocalypse Now*, without the helicopters . . .' Now, however, it sounded somehow much more final. Bono was rumored to be working on a book of poetry, Larry was said to be working on a book about injuries suffered by rock musicians, The Edge apparently wanted to plough millions into a chain of traditional hardware and DIY stores across Ireland, and Adam, it was reported, just wanted to renovate his stately home just outside Dublin.

Even Bono was now saying things like: 'If you spend too long in America you get sick of the constant hard sell. The first thing I do when I get home is order a pint of Guinness because it's real, and then listen to some traditional music. Doing this helps remind me of what normal life is about. I'm not from the limousine/private jet/luxury hotel type of world which has become part of the territory with U2.'

Amid all this U2 had become £30 million richer when Island sold out to the music giant Polygram.

For the first few months of 1990 Bono, The Edge, Adam, and Larry threw themselves into their home lives in Dublin. They had resisted all pressures to leave their home town and were still familiar sights browsing around the shops and bars of O'Connell Street and Grafton Street. They were also keen to devote time to Mother Records, the label they had formed to encourage and record Irish talent. They had released singles by the Hothouse Flowers and In Tua Nua.

On the personal front, Bono and Ali, who had had their first baby daughter in May 1989, were rumored to have hired a £300-an-hour helicopter to go house-hunting in County

LEFT: After the roasting U2 received over *Rattle and Hum* it seemed suddenly questionable that they were 'The Greatest Show on Earth.'

Dublin. They eventually settled on a nine-bedroomed Victorian mansion with sweeping views to the sea in an area known locally as Beverly Hills.

The Edge, who in 1983 had married his youthful sweetheart, Aislinn, was also a father (he would go on to have three daughters) and had bought a grand home, surrounded by a nine-foot security wall, in a seaside resort south of Dublin.

Larry lived in a rock star's home in Howth and Adam had bought a fortified mansion in the foothills of Rathfarnham, South Dublin.

Their only real brush with publicity came in February when Anthony Burgess, author of *A Clockwork Orange*, attacked the music they had specially penned for the Royal Shakespeare Company's production of his work. It just couldn't compare to the Beethoven he intended to be heard. 'He should stick to writing. That's what he's good at' snapped Bono.

In October they emerged from exile briefly to contribute a song and a video to the Red, Hot and Blue project to raise money for Aids charities. All the artists involved were asked to do a cover of a Cole Porter song. U2 chose a dance-orientated version of *Night and Day*.

Shortly afterwards, and again in early 1991, the band journeyed to Berlin to begin working on a new album at the

ABOVE LEFT: **U2 outside the Chinese Theater in Los Angeles while promoting the film *Rattle and Hum*.**

BELOW LEFT: **An unusually besuited Adam Clayton for the promotion at the Chinese Theater.**

ABOVE: **The Edge outside St Basil's Cathedral in Red Square.**

RIGHT: **Bono leaving celebrity haunt Langan's Brasserie in London, with wife Ali.**

legendary Hansa by the Wall studios where Brian Eno had helped David Bowie craft the *Low* and *Heroes* albums in 1976 and 1977.

The making of the album was not without its tensions. The Edge's marriage had broken up and he was desolate and worrying all over again about reconciling his fame with his belief in God.

Speaking in veiled terms about the break-up, The Edge said: 'The worst thing about being on the road is coming home and spending two months of cold turkey trying to pick up the threads of the life you had before you left. You spend a long time finding normal life very weird.' In the wake of this personal calamity The Edge talked of leaving U2. 'If you do I'll break the band up' said Bono.

The angst was eventually resolved, said Bono, by 'splitting up the band and then reforming it with the same members.' In the studio they struggled to rediscover that 'spark' that had brought them together in the first place. 'It was so hard, so heavy making that album that we thought maybe we really should break up. Luckily we manage to ride the storm and produce a great album, but for a long time the magic just wasn't there' recalled The Edge.

Paul McGuinness was at his most ruthlessly astute in these months, imposing a Press blackout and trying to steer the band away from the kind of over-exposure that had soured

TOP: **The band during the making of *Rattle and Hum*. They would soon ignore America for three years because of the savaging the film and its companion double album was to receive at the hands of critics in the States.**

ABOVE: **'When I was on the West Coast I was almost allergic to people. . . . I was a commodity – bought, sold, and then redundant. It was like *Apocalypse Now* without the helicopters' said Bono.**

RIGHT: **The Edge arrives at New York's Waldorf Hotel for the 7th Rock 'n' Roll Hall of Fame Induction Dinner.**

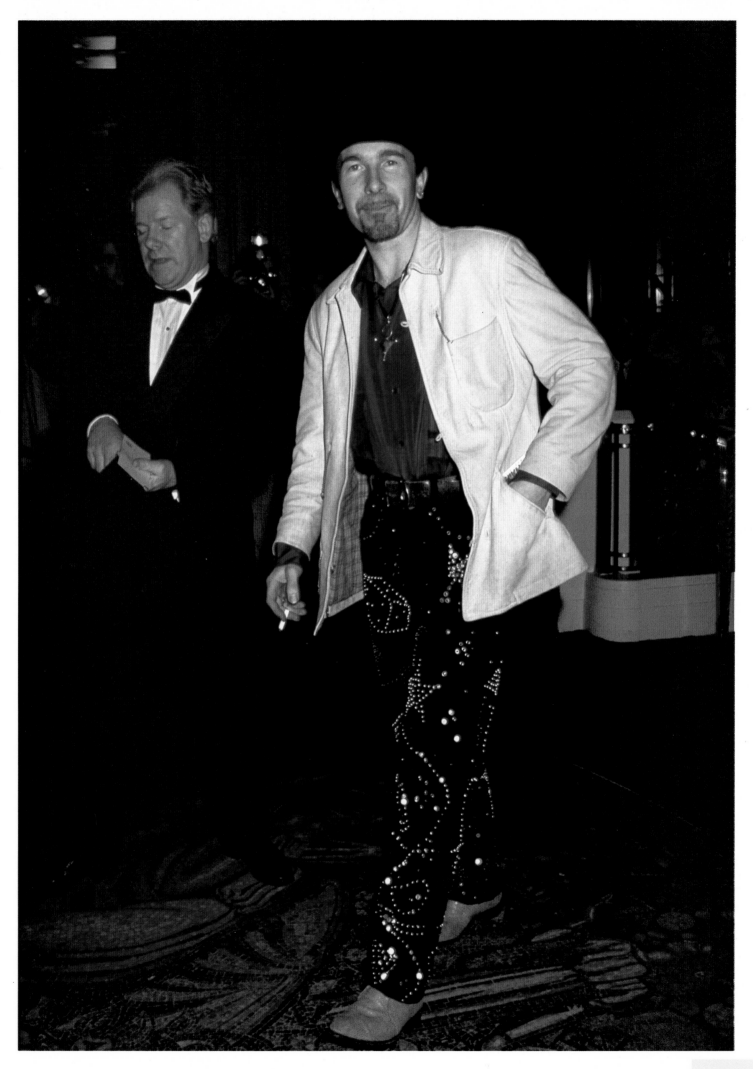

LEFT: After *Rattle and Hum* Adam joined the others in going back to Dublin to lick his wounds; he said 'if you spend too much time in America you get tired of the constant hard sell. I'm not from the limousine/private jet/luxury hotel kind of world which has become part of the territory with U2.' But soon he would be reboarding the private jets with renewed relish as the band emerged from the doldrums and reinvented themselves for their next album *Achtung Baby*.

RIGHT: Gone are the days of the Bible-bashing, long-haired Messiah. Wearing wraparound glasses, greased-back hair, and tight leather trousers, Bono is reincarnated as The Fly.

FOLLOWING PAGES: The view from the stage in Miami, Florida, for one of just 31 hit-and-run concerts in U2's Zoo TV tour of 1992 to promote their masterpiece *Achtung Baby*. Fluorescently painted Trabant cars hang from the ceiling, in keeping with the album's recording in post-communist Berlin.

things for them in the States. In October 1991, and with very little fanfair, he announced that the new single would only be on sale for three weeks in order 'to get it out of the way for the next one.' Though some attacked this marketing ploy as 'cynical manipulation' it was no surprise that the single, *The Fly*, shot straight into the British and American charts at #1.

The album, *Achtung Baby*, was hailed as a masterpiece by the critics. The sound of Bono's voice was often deliberately distorted, The Edge's guitar took on an air of menace. The goody-goody image was dead and buried, here was an album that took its influences from hip-hop to Kurt Weill. Asked what it sounded like, Bono said: 'Well, to me, it's the sound of four men chopping down *The Joshua Tree*.'

The glib title hinted at a change of direction too. There was nothing earnest in it any more and the cover was not the usual arty solo shot but a chaotic patchwork of 'snapshots' – some in black and white shot in Berlin mixed with color photographs shot in Morocco and Ireland. It even included a full-frontal nude shot of Adam.

The band who had been hailed, and later attacked, as Messiahs seemed determined now to play the Devil – after all, he has all the best tunes. Within weeks of its release *Achtung Baby* had sold seven million copies worldwide – and it had rescued their careers and credibility in America.

On 29 February 1992 U2 returned to the American stage for the first time in just over four years with a concert in Lakeland, Florida. The tickets for the show in the relatively small 6000-seater stadium had sold out in just three minutes. McGuinness had conceived the Zoo TV Station tour, as it was known, as a hit-and-run affair. The band would play just one night in each city, give few interviews, and move on. Learning from the mistakes following *The Joshua Tree* and *Rattle and Hum*, he had learned the hard way the truth of that old showbusiness adage about leaving them crying for more . . . and that's exactly what happened as the whirlwind tour hit 31 cities, ending up in Vancouver on 23 April.

'We've deliberately made this a hard ticket to get. The audience who are most exciting to play for, and contribute to a great show, are those people who really want to be there. A readily-available ticket leads to a dull audience' explained McGuinness.

His tactics worked brilliantly. In the midst of a recession, you couldn't give tickets away for stadium acts like Genesis and Dire Straits as they lugged their worn-out shows across America. There were no empty seats for U2.

The stage show marked a dramatic change of direction as well. Having spent most of the Eighties trying to play down the rock-star image Bono now looked like a man making up

for lost time. His new stage persona was unashamedly camp. He wore black leather for the first half, a silver lamé suit for the second, his hair was slicked back and he wore wraparound sunglasses. He swiveled his hips, showered the audience with champagne, pinched The Edge's bottom, kissed Adam's cheek, and trained a camcorder on his crotch as the image was simultaneously projected on to huge screens above the stage in a blatant display of narcissism. The irony was intentional but all the same it often looked like pure Presley.

For the first time U2 used electronic wizardry. Six luminously painted Trabants (the infamous East German car) hung from the ceiling and images from bison running to soft porn played on the screens, interrupted by flashes of slogans with messages like: 'Conscience Is A Pest, Sex, Call Your Mother, I'd Like To Teach The World To Sing, Death Is A Career Move, Everything You Know Is Wrong.' It was a perfect comment on the media-obsessed Nineties.

Other gimmicks included making live 'phone calls on stage. Bono dialed a sex-talk line, tried to link-up with a Russian astronaut in space – and even called the White House. And he writhed on a catwalk with a belly dancer while performing *she moves in mysterious ways.*

After Europe, the tour hit Britain. Stories began emerging about Larry's hands. He had been diagnosed as

LEFT: Mad, bad, and dangerous to know – Bono seemed to be lapping up his new camp rock 'n' roll image in the persona of The Fly.

TOP AND ABOVE: During the Zoo TV show Bono switched from black leather to silver lamé and indulged in a joyous display of showbiz narcissism which many described as being pure Presley. He made live phone calls during the show – from anything to a sex line to George Bush, then President, at the White House.

FAR LEFT: Now recognized as an accomplished bass player, Adam Clayton seems to have made all his teenage dreams come true. He was a rebel with a cause after all.

ABOVE: A concert in Miami – the band of the eighties now seems set to conquer the nineties.

LEFT: After many years of battling with his conscience the price of fame has indeed been high for The Edge. He has now split up with his wife and youthful sweetheart Aislinn.

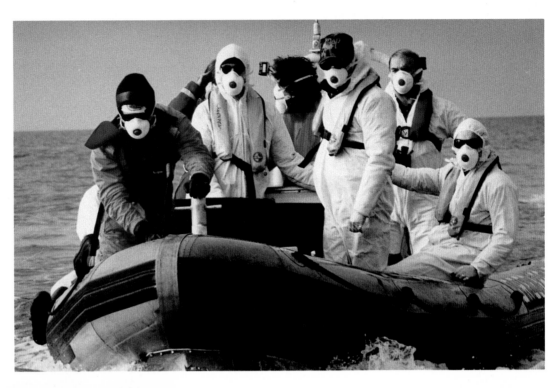

RIGHT: In June 1992 U2 joined a Greenpeace protest at Sellafield nuclear power station after original plans to play a free concert were banned by the High Court. Traveling in dinghies they delivered drums of allegedly polluted mud from Irish beaches to the perimeters of Sellafield.

BELOW: Bono at a Press Conference for Zoo TV.

LEFT: Bono on stage as the leather-clad Fly. Asked what the metallic-sounding *Achtung Baby* sounded like 'Well, to me, its the sound of four men chopping down the Joshua Tree.'

FOLLOWING PAGES: They started with punk-inspired rock, moved on to lyrical, anthemic, and epic tunes, flirted with rock 'n' roll roots they were hardly old enough to understand, enjoyed phenomenal success and vitriolic recrimination but have now reclaimed their place as the 'Saviors of Rock 'n' Roll.'

suffering from 'piano hand' – a frequent injury for musicians – and had undergone surgery to try to correct it. Every drum roll would cause him excrutiating pain. He had taken to wearing a special support glove. Though the tabloids made much of the line that doctors had warned him that if he carried on he 'would never play again,' Larry seemed in thunderous form when they played to a rapturous audience at London's vast Earl's Court in June of that year.

Also that month they took part in a much-publicised Greenpeace protest at the Sellafield nuclear powerstation in north-west England. The original plans to play a concert on the site were banned in the High Court. Instead the band wore radiation suits and carried drums of allegedly polluted mud from Irish beaches to the perimeters of Sellafield 2. 'They can call us mad Paddies if they want to, but we can't put a lot of faith in politicians' said Bono.

Four more hit singles were released from the album – *She Moves in Mysterious Ways*, *One*, *Even Better Than The Real Thing* and *Who's Gonna Ride Your Wild Horses*.

What U2 accomplished with *Achtung Baby* might have been considered impossible. Like that other Messiah, they had risen from a kind of grave. Now the critics were happy, the fans were happy, the band had come to terms with its success and were reveling in it. More, they had stayed together. Bono had often talked of being the heart of the band, while The Edge was the head and Adam and Larry were the legs. As individuals, he was saying, they may be nothing extraordinary, but as a unit they were truly the stuff of which legends are made. The band of the Eighties had proved that they just might also be the band of the Nineties.

Not bad for a bunch of yobbos from Dublin . . .

DISCOGRAPHY UK SINGLES

Out of Control/Stories for Boys/Boy-Girl
(CBS, only in Ireland) September 1979

Another Day/Twilight
(CBS, only in Ireland) February 1980

11 O'Clock Tick Tock/Touch
(Island) August 1980

A Day Without Me/Things to Make And Do
(Island) August 1980

I Will Follow/Boy-Girl
(Island) October 1980

Fire/J. Swallo (7") *11 O'Clock Tick Tock/The Ocean* (12") *Cry/ The Electric Co./11 O'Clock Tick Tock/The Ocean* (7" Double Pack)
(Island) June 1981. Highest Chart Position: #35

Gloria/I Will Follow
(Island) October 1981. Highest Chart Position: #55

A Celebration/Trash, Trampoline and The Party Girl
(Island) October 1982. Highest Chart Position: #47

New Year's Day/Treasure (7") *Fire/I Threw A Brick Through A Window/*
A Day Without Me (7" Double Pack)
(Island) January 1983. Highest Chart Position: #10

Two Hearts Beat As One/Endless Deep (7") *Two Hearts Beat As One/*
New Year's Day (12" and Double Pack)
(Island) March 1983. Highest Chart Position: #18

Pride (In The Name Of Love)/Boomerang (7") *Boomerang 11/4th of July* (12")
(Island) September 1984. Highest Chart Position: #3

Do They Know It's Christmas?
(Phonogram) December 1984. Highest Chart Position: #1*
Featuring Bono only on Live Aid charity single, written by Bob Geldof and Midge Ure.

The Unforgettable Fire/A Sort of Homecoming (7") *The Three Sunrises/*
Love Comes Tumbling (12") *Love Comes Tumbling/Sixty Seconds in Kingdom Come* (7" Double Pack)
(Island) April 1985. Highest Chart Position: #6

With or Without You/Luminous Times (Hold On To Love)/Walk To The Water
(Island) March 1987.
Highest Chart Position: #4

I Still Haven't Found What I'm Looking For/Spanish Eyes/Deep In The Heart
(Island) May 1987. Highest Chart Position: #6

Where The Streets Have No Name/Silver and Gold/Sweetest Thing
(Island) August 1987. Highest Chart Position: #4

Desire/Hallelujah (Here She Comes (7") *Desire* (12" Hollywood Mix)
(Island) September 1988

Angel of Harlem/A Room At The Heartbreak Hote (7") *Me* (12" and CD with Keith Richards and Ziggy Marley*((Island) December 1988. Highest Chart Position: #9

When Love Comes To Town/Dancing Barefoot (7") *When Love Comes To Town/God Par II* (12")
(Island) April 1989. Highest Chart Position: #6

All I Want Is You/Unchained Melody (7") *Everlasting Love* (12" and CD)
(Island) June 1989. Highest Chart Position: #4

Night And Day (Limited editions only, taken from the Aids benefit/ Cole Porter tribute album, *Red, Hot and Blue*)
December 1990

The Fly/Alex Descends Into Hell For A Bottle Of Milk (7") *The Lounge Fly Mix* (12" and CD)
(Island) October 1991. Highest Chart Position: #1

Mysterious Ways/Mysterious Ways (Solar Plexus Magic Hour Remix) (7") *Solar Plexus Extended Club Mix/Apollo 440 Magic Hour Remix/ Tamla Motown Remix/Solar Plexus Club Mix* (12" and CD)
(Island) December 1991. Highest Chart Position: #13

One
(Island) Febuary 1992. Highest Chart Position: #6

Even Better Than The Real Thing
(Island) June 1992. Highest Chart Position: #8

Who's Gonna Ride Your Wild Horses
(Island) November (23) 1992. Highest Chart Position: # 14

DISCOGRAPHY US SINGLES

I Will Follow/Out of Control.
April 1981

New Year's Day/Treasure.
February 1983

Two Hearts Beat As One/Endless Deep.
June 1983

I Will Follow/Two Hearts Beat As One.
January 1984

Pride/Boomerang II.
October 1984

New Year's Day/Two Hearts Beat As One.
Re-release, 1983

Sunday Bloody Sunday/Gloria.
Re-release, 1985

Pride/ I Will Follow.
Re-release, 1985

With Or Without You/Luminous Times/Walk To The Water.
March 1987

*I Still Haven't Found What I'm Looking For/Spanish Eyes/Deep In
The Heart.*
May 1987

Where The Streets Have No Name/Silver and Gold/Sweetest Thing.
August 1987

In God's Country/Bullet The Blue Sky/Running To Stand Still
November 1987

Desire/Hallelujah Here She Comes
September 1988

Angel of Harlem/A Room At The Heartbreak Hotel.
December 1988

When Love Comes To Town/Dancing Barefoot.
March 1989

All I Want Is You/Unchained Melody.
June 1989

*The Fly/The Fly (The Lounge Fly Mix)/
Alex Descends Into Hell For A Bottle Of Milk.*
October 1991

*Mysterious Ways/Mysterious Ways (Solar Plexus Extended Club
Mix)/Mysterious Ways (Apollo 440 Magic Hour Remix)/Mysterious
Ways
(Tamla Motown Remix)/Mysterious Ways (Solar Plexus Club Mix).*
November 1991

*One/Lady With The Spinning Head/Satellite of Love/Night and Day
(Steel String Remix).*
March 1992

DISCOGRAPHY ALBUMS

BOY
(Island) October 1981. Highest Chart Position: #11

OCTOBER
(Island) October 1981. Highest Chart Position: #11

WAR
(Island) March 1983. Highest Chart Position: #1

UNDER A BLOOD RED SKY
(Island) June 1983.

THE UNFORGETTABLE FIRE
(Island) October 1984: Highest Chart Position: #1

THE JOSHUA TREE
(Island) March 1987. Highest Chart Position: #1

RATTLE AND HUM
(Island) October 1980. Highest Chart Position: #1

ACHTUNG BABY
(Island) November 1991. Highest Chart Position: #1

All albums also released simultaneously in US, except Boy, which was released in America in
January 1981

Index

ACKNOWLEDGMENTS

The publisher would like to thank Alan Gooch and Ron Callow of Design 23 who designed this book, Pat Coward who prepared the index, and Rita Longabucco, the picture researcher. We would also like to thank the following agencies and individuals for supplying the illustrations:

CAMERA PRESS: page 43 (below right)/J WATSON: 64 (above); RON GALLELA LTD/ARROYA: page 62 (above)/KELLY JORDAN: 65/ O'CONNOR: 55 (below)/ANTHONY SAVIGNANO: 45; CLAUDE GASSIAN: pages 1, 7, 10 (right), 12, 16-17, 17 (above), 18 (both), 21 (both), 22-23, 24 (both), 25, 26, 28 (below), 29, 30, 43 (above right), 44-45, 45 (both), 49, 50-51 (all three), 55 (above), 56-57, 59 (below), 78-79; GLOBE PHOTOS/JOHN BARRETT: page 58; CHARLES MCQUILLAN: page 66; PICTORIAL PRESS LTD: pages 6-7, 32-33, 35, 37, 38, 42 (below), 43 (left), 44 (left), 54, 59 (above), 63 (below)/STEVE CALLAGHAN: 40-41, 42 (above)/SVENSON: 70; RETNA PICTURES LTD/ADRIAN BOOT: pages 16 (above), 19, 27 (both), 28 (both), 63 (above), 75 (both)/LARRY BUSACCA: 4-5, 71 (both), 74, 76-77/BILL DAVILA: 73 (below)/STEVE DOUBLE: 60-61, 67/ GARY GERSHOFF: 36-37, 39, 52-53 (both)/STEVE GRANITZ: 62 (below), 64 (below)/ANDREA LAUBACH: 34 (both)/ CLIFF LIPSON: 46-47/STEVE RAPPORT: 10 (LEFT), 11 (LEFT), 17 (BELOW), 31/ ART SEITZ: 68-69, 73 (above)/PAUL SLATTERY: 8-9, 11 (right), 13, 14-15, 20/STILLS: 2-3/SCOTT WEINER: 72